I DON'T THINK SO

Leaving Behind the
Why Me
Mentality and
Taking Control
of Your Life

Melanie Mitchell

Please note that Evangelista Media™ publishing style does not capitalize the name satan and related names. We choose not to acknowledge him, even to the point of violating grammatical rules.

Cover Design: Chantelle Cook

EVANGELISTA MEDIA™ srl
Via Maiella, 1
66020 San Giovanni Teatino (Ch) – Italy

"Changing the World, One Book at a Time."

This book and all other Evangelista Media™ books are available at Christian bookstores and distributors worldwide.

To order products, or for any other correspondence:

EVANGELISTA MEDIA™ srl
Via della Scafa, 29/14
65013 Città Sant'Angelo – Italy
Tel. +39 085 4716623 • Fax: +39 085 9090113
Email: info@evangelistamedia.com
Or reach us on the Internet: www.evangelistamedia.com

ISBN 13: 978-88-97896-51-7
ISBN EBOOK: 978-88-97896-53-1

For Worldwide Distribution, Printed in Canada
1 2 3 4 5 6 / 16 15 14 13

DEDICATION

This book is lovingly dedicated to my son.

ACKNOWLEDGMENTS

This book is my way of saying thank you.

Thank you so much to my cherished son and daughter-in-law for cheering me on and supporting me in this project. Your excitement has meant the world to me. I love you both immensely, and I am so thankful to have you in my life. Children sometimes pay a higher price for our mistakes than we do ourselves; and my son, you paid a high price for mine. Thank you for your courage and the honorable way you have chosen to live your life. You have chosen well and are building a great future. You truly are an overcomer. I am so proud of you and the incredible man you have become. When it was difficult for me to keep pushing through to freedom, you were always my motivation to keep going. You were always worth fighting for. I can't change the past, but I am hopeful that this book will change the future for others, enabling them to find freedom and escape the pain and loss that our family experienced because we didn't know any other way.

Thank you to everyone who walked with me on my journey and helped me find freedom—this story is your story, too. From my amazing family—my sister, my parents, and my grandparents who endlessly supported me and loved me every step of the way—to those who led me to Christ, discipled me, prayed for me, befriended me, pastored me, and taught me how to walk in God's ways, I wouldn't be where I am today without you.

A special thank you goes to my wonderful team of friends, Connie Thomson and Esther and Len Gillingham, who spent many evenings reading and rereading my manuscript. Thank you for being a safe place to share the deepest parts of my heart. I truly appreciate your dedication and commitment to this project. We shared some good laughs and some heartfelt tears, and I will never think about exclamation marks or commas the same way again. You made working fun.

Thank you to Dian Layton, my friend and mentor who encouraged me, taught me, and guided me, and became a closer and dearer friend in the process. Not only did you diligently edit my manuscript multiple times over, but you were there whenever I needed advice or assistance. Late at night, when everyone else was sleeping, you were up with me getting the job done. I couldn't have done it without you. Thank you for your expertise that helped make my book the best it could be. You are amazing.

Thank You Jesus for everything You have done for me and for the freedom I have come to know. Not only did You lay down Your life for me, but You took the ashes of my broken life and turned them into something beautiful. I never cease to be amazed by Your unending love and how it changes me. Thank You for setting me free and giving me a greater life than I could have ever dreamed of. I love You, my Lord and my King.

ENDORSEMENTS

So many people struggle through life, caught in circumstances and wondering why bad things have happened to them. Melanie Mitchell's book *I Don't Think So* speaks to the heart of the matter. It teaches readers how to change their thinking so that they can take control of their lives and begin to live the way God created them to live. Not only does Melanie give readers hope that life can be different, she walks them through the process required to make it happen. I am so excited to see such a practical and insightful book that empowers people to walk out of captivity and into the freedom of the life they have dreamed of. I believe it will change the lives of many.

Tommy Barnett
Senior Pastor, Phoenix First Assembly
Founder, Los Angeles Dream Center

Have you ever wondered how to change where you are today in order to bring about a different tomorrow? This book gives you the right tools in your toolbox to replace thoughts in your mind of rejection, abuse, terror, disappointments, and pain that have trapped your mindset. Melanie writes, "Anytime someone is taken captive by a person, an addiction, or a circumstance, it is because they developed a mindset that gave jurisdiction over their life to their captor." Moving forward in life you need to know where to start. This book will equip you to move out of being a victim into living a life of a champion. Through her story she shows you how to change your mind in order to change your life.

Sheila Gerald
Champions Centre

I Don't Think So is courageous. It's one thing to escape from physical captivity, but mental and spiritual captivity present entirely different challenges. Through vulnerability and sound Bible teaching, Melanie equips those who struggle with a victim mentality to get free. As Melanie says, "Liberation comes from the very heart of God," and *I Don't Think So* illustrates His ability to set people free in the face of the most difficult circumstances.

Steve Murrell, President
Every Nation Churches & Ministries

When I met Melanie Mitchell seventeen years ago, she was a broken person. I watched her make decisions and choose the life of principles presented in *I Don't Think So* for a new way of life. With a positive faith, she models what life and leadership are all about. I highly recommend *I Don't Think So* as a resource to help you make your life a better life.

Mel C. Mullen
Founding Pastor, Word of Life Church
Red Deer, Alberta, Canada

I first met Melanie Mitchell when she was beginning her journey to wholeness. Since then, she has become an overcomer, a champion, and a personal friend. Melanie identified and overcame some hidden enemies and went from personal captivity into a great freedom that everyone is meant to enjoy. In my world I see many people who are held captive by their thinking and traditions who need the freedom found in this book. It is full of wisdom, encouragement, powerful insights, and life-changing principles that will help every person take control of their thoughts and their lives.

Brian Thomson
Author, Director of Home of Hope

It takes great courage and vulnerability to tell your story. It also takes bravery to move from living in the clutches of a victim mentality to walking into total freedom. Every person will either live their lives by default or by design based on their individual choices. Melanie shares both her heartbreaking story and triumphant journey into freedom, giving the reader powerful tools and motivation to move forward in life as well. I highly recommend this book as a great tool for living a victorious life in Christ.

Helen Burns
Pastor, Relate Church
Author, Television Host
Surrey, British Columbia

From a life held hostage by helplessness to the joy of freedom, Melanie's inspiring and transformational book shows you a way out of pain and struggle and reveals the truth of who you really are.

Fran Hewitt
Author, *The Power of Focus for Women*
and *The Ego and the Spirit*

We all go through tough times, and these tough times actually have the power to define us. The definition will be either as victims or something totally, radically different! Melanie tells us about a powerful life truth through the pages of her new book *I Don't Think So.* It is a must read!

Melanie Mitchell is a brilliant communicator and her new book takes us from having a victim mentality to one where we decided to take responsibility in life and learn to respond to the tough stuff life hands out to us. None of us are immune to troubles, trials, or tribulations, but we can decide not to become victims living lackluster lives forever. This is not what God intended for us—Melanie shares this truth so well. I urge you to read this book and buy copies for your friends.

Tom Rawls
Lead Pastor, Proclaimers
Norwich, England

I Don't Think So boldly confronts the trap of a victim mentality that robs many people of the life God intended for them. Through her own courageous story, Melanie teaches readers how to recognize this mindset in their own lives. She goes on to provide them with practical steps to free themselves from captivity and take control of their lives. Melanie is truly an overcomer and will lead many to freedom and victory through this powerful book.

Joe Champion
Pastor, Celebration Church
Georgetown, Texas

CONTENTS

FOREWORD

Life is the most precious gift the Lord has given us. We are called to prosper and lead a fulfilled existence. However, even the most devoted Christian will face difficulty, heartbreak, pain, and sorrow. There are so many blessings that the Lord places in our lives, but when trials and setbacks occur, it is so easy to lose focus of the amazing blessings He has given us. We are all human, and we all fall short of the glory of God. Although we all experience depression and helplessness, it is harmful to stay in such mindsets.

There is nothing more powerful than hope, and the lack of hope can destroy people from the inside out, robbing them of their true potential. The Lord is at work all around us, guiding us and shaping us. Life will come with difficulty, but such things are not meant to last. The trials and setbacks we go through are meant to teach us lessons and build our character, bringing us closer to God.

For many people, it seems impossible to escape a life of heartbreak. I have met so many people with amazing potential and the most genuine personalities, but they are stuck in a cycle of hopelessness and despair. Freedom is so near to these people, but it is a concept that seems impossible to them. Once people give in to despair, it can grow and overtake their lives. A victim mentality is corrosive to the soul, and it can be very hard to escape, like quicksand pulling you down.

The good news is that the redemptive power of God's love is available to all of us. Even if the negative mindset seems to be overpowering, it is still possible to change your way of thinking, take control of your life, and flourish in the comfort that God's hand is at work in your life. As it says in Philippians 4:13, "I can do all things through Christ who strengthens me" (NKJV). God's grace is welcome to all of us. When you become aware of the victim mentality, it can be overcome.

Melanie Mitchell is a living testimony of how the presence of God can break down a victim mentality and restore a person to greatness. She has gone through more heartbreak than anyone should have to deal with; and although it felt like her life was being hijacked, the Lord never left her side. Through her life experiences and years of service to the ministry, she has helped others overcome the circumstances that tried to rob them of their joy. Melanie Mitchell has a true talent for using her past and the lessons she learned to enrich her own life as well as the lives of many others.

Pastor Matthew Barnett
Cofounder, Dream Center

Chapter 1

HIJACKED NO MORE

He felt as though he couldn't breathe. The air was stagnant, and he couldn't move. His hands and feet had been bound for hours now. He could feel his atrophied muscles screaming to be released, but it seemed hopeless. He had never felt so powerless or so afraid. He was unaware of how much time had passed; twenty-four hours, thirty-six hours, more? It seemed like forever. He could hear time dragging painfully by as the clock on the wall behind him clicked with the passing of each single second. Tick, tick, tick. Other than that there was only the ominous sound of silence or the occasional whimper or groan coming from one of the other hostages. No one dared protest; their lives were at stake.

It had all happened so fast. He was on his way home from work, just like any other day, when he decided to make a quick stop at the bank. Nothing seemed out of the ordinary as he waited in line, thinking about the evening ahead with his family. Then, out of nowhere it happened. He hadn't suspected a thing was wrong until he felt the hard metal barrel of a gun being shoved into his back and heard a man's voice yelling in his ear, commanding people to get down on the floor. One moment everything was fine, and the next moment he was a hostage. His life was no longer his own. It seemed surreal to think it had really happened. Yesterday's freedom was a distant memory. He faded in and out of sleep. When he woke up, he would tell himself that it must have been a bad dream... But then he opened his eyes and saw the masked man with the gun who couldn't be reasoned with. The man who had stolen his freedom and threatened his life. The hijacker.

✦✦✦

Whenever a hijacking takes place, everyone involved comes to a quick conclusion—"Stop the hijacking." Both the victims and those called on for help recognize that lives are in jeopardy, and they begin to act as quickly as possible to bring the hijacking to an end. In some instances, complete strangers become comrades, united in their determination to take back control from the hijacker and free the hostages. When the hijacking ends, the people who went up against the hijackers are lauded as heroes because they confronted the enemy and freed the victims. In the hearts of those who were watching and waiting, there is a sense that all is well with the world again. Liberation of any prisoner always brings celebration, because liberation comes from the very heart of God. People rejoice when captives are freed!

But what about ordinary people who have never been physically hijacked? What about people who are taken hostage by abuse, addiction, poverty, tragedy, or sickness? What about those whose lives are hijacked without them even knowing that a crime has been committed against them? It might not be a crime in the eyes of the law, but it is a crime in God's eyes. They have never been taken hostage or had a gun held to their heads, but they are still held captive. They are unable to live in the freedom and enjoyment God created for them. We don't hear the names of those people on the news, and we probably don't give them a second glance in the grocery store or at the bank, but they are prisoners. Their lives are lived in captivity. Shouldn't they be entitled to freedom, too?

Isaiah 58:6 reads, *"...Free those who are wrongly imprisoned; lighten the burden of those who work for you. Let the oppressed go free, and remove the chains that bind people."* This Scripture is not referring to random events where a plane is hijacked by a terrorist or a bank is robbed and someone with a weapon takes innocent people hostage. It is talking about people whose emotional, spiritual, or relational lives are imprisoned, oppressed, and bound. They live every day in this condition with no hope of freedom. For them, captivity is not an occurrence or an event; it is a way of life. If you know any of them, you know that they live as if there is an invisible gun being held to their heads, making them unable to choose what they want. They have seemingly been stripped of their freedom of choice.

These victims refer to their hijacker, whether it is abuse, disease, or poverty, as *circumstances*. They do not know any other way to live except *under the circumstances*. If you ask them how they are, they will qualify their answer with *"Under the circumstances...."* If you invite them to do something, usually they will tell you that they are unable to *"...under the circumstances."* At the very least, they will tell you they have to check with their hijacker first. They say they will see if they have the money, or they will see if they are feeling well enough. The way they talk about their lives reveals that something has taken control and is ruling over them. They do not go anywhere without their hijacker; it doesn't let them.

Some people are hostages to abusive parents or spouses. Others are hostages to poverty or sickness. Still others are captured by the power of alcohol, drugs, or gambling. Some are destroyed by divorce. In every case, something people encounter hijacks them and takes charge. They begin living each day under its rule. Their choices and decisions are based on what their hijacker demands.

It is easy to identify when a physical hijacking is taking place; everyone recognizes it instantly. There is a hijacker, a weapon, and a demand. But when individual lives are hijacked, the alarm system that should detect the presence of an enemy has been disarmed, and the victims do not identify what is happening. If they did, they would react. Instead of trying to stop it, they embrace it, thinking, *This is just life.* They may even believe that they deserve or are the cause of what has happened and falsely conclude that they have no right to take action. That false belief empowers the hijacker, securing its place of authority in the person's life.

No one plans to get hijacked; I certainly didn't. I didn't plan to get divorced. I didn't plan to lose custody of my son. I didn't plan to lose my friends, my home, and my reputation. I was the girl most likely to succeed, but success turned to failure when I married a man and gave my life over to his control. Life became cruel and harsh, and instead of recognizing that something was wrong, I believed with all sincerity that what was happening to me was my fault. I thought I deserved it. My life was hijacked and I began to live each day in captivity.

In the beginning I wasn't looking for help or a way out because I didn't know that a hijacking was taking place. As time passed, I accepted that there was no way of escape and no hope of change. I was imprisoned by pain, oppressed by hopelessness, and bound by chains I could not see. When reality became too painful, I disengaged my heart and escaped to a world of numbness. It was easier not to feel. Eventually, I became nothing more than a shell of a person, unable to truly connect with the people around me and unable to carry on a conversation for more than a few minutes at a time. No one knew about the tragic world I lived within myself.

How did my life get hijacked? Why did it happen to me? Why does this subversive hijacking continue in the lives of so many people? Why don't people react the same way as they would if they were being hijacked on an airplane? Why don't they resist the hijacker? Why don't they cry for help? The reason is that the enemy does not have a face, a name, or a gun. It is unseen. It is difficult to recognize an invisible enemy. By the time you can identify it, it is too late. It has already taken control.

It took years before I identified the enemy in my life; and when I did, I realized exactly how I became a victim. The truth opened the prison doors that I had been living behind, and I walked away free. I am not living a hijacked life anymore. The hijackers are gone, pain and hopelessness are long forgotten, and no one is holding an invisible gun to my head. It is not because I got a divorce or because someone rescued me. It is because I recognized my real enemy and faced it; as a result I am now living in freedom instead of captivity. I am the one in charge of my life. I am free. Free to choose. Free to live. Free to love. Free to create. Free to give. Free to dream. My life has been liberated.

I am thankful every day for the freedom I have come to know. I love my life and enjoy the experience and opportunity that each day brings. Jesus said, *"A thief is only there to steal and kill and destroy. I came so they can have real and eternal life, more and better life than they ever dreamed of"* (John 10:10 MSG). That's the kind of life I am now living, the life Jesus intended for me.

I am not satisfied to have found this freedom for myself; I want others to know it, too. That is the heart with which I wrote this book. It is not to blame, accuse, or judge anyone; it is to share my story and the process God led me through from captivity into freedom. I have shared these thoughts countless times in ordinary conversations with people who found themselves hijacked in one way or another—people who needed help to untangle themselves from lies they believed and take back control of their lives. I have cheered them on as they recognized their own enemies, faced them head-on, and freed themselves from the chains binding them. In the same way, I believe my story will allow you to recognize any areas where you have been hijacked. As you walk through the practical steps outlined in the book, you will be empowered to recognize and overcome the beliefs that laid the groundwork for a hijacked lifestyle and way of thinking. This process will release you from captivity and teach you how to take control of your life.

Hijacked? *I don't think so.*

Chapter 2

CAPTIVITY BEGINS WITH A THOUGHT

Things happen to all of us that were never intended to happen. But it is not the event or the experience that defines us, it is *how we respond* to that event or experience. In fact, our response to what happens is far more critical than what actually happens. That is why some people can experience incredible trauma and come out unscathed, while others experience a good life yet success eludes them.

Everyone's journey is different, but the Bible teaches us that everyone faces temptations: *"The temptations in your life are no different from what others experience. And God is faithful. He will not allow the temptation to be more than you can stand. When you are tempted, he will show you a way out so that you can endure"* (1 Corinthians 10:13). In other words, no matter what happens, there is a way to respond that protects us from being hijacked or destroyed by the negative experiences of life.

Although our responses differ, they are not random, unexplainable, or a matter of character. They are a matter of thought. Our thoughts determine our responses, so how we think about what happens to us determines how it will affect our lives. *Captivity begins with a thought.*

It is vital that we know the way out of temptation, the way to think that will protect us from captivity. How we think about our value or worth is a critical factor in determining how we will respond to what happens to us. If we have a good sense of self-worth, then we will process negative events or experiences. It may take us time to heal or recover, but we will move past those experiences without being hijacked by them. In contrast, if we have a poor sense of self-worth, negative events will cripple us and lock us in time, leaving us unable to move on or change the circumstances.

Here is an example. If I have a brand-new, crisp twenty-dollar bill, I know what its value is. I understand what I could purchase with it. It is not an opinion that I have; it is a fact. I had nothing to do with determining the value of the twenty-dollar bill; that was determined by its creator, enforced by government, and cannot be altered. If I mistreat the money by dropping it in the mud and stepping on it so it becomes dirty and crumpled, its value does not change. It is still a twenty-dollar bill, and it still has the same worth. It might not be received with the same welcome as it would have before it got mistreated, but its value remains constant and its identity is unchanged. I can still accomplish the same things with it. There is nothing I can do to it to make it worth less.

Every person is created the same way—with value. Our value was determined by our Creator. God chose to give us life and that life was given in love. His gift is what determines our value. We cannot do anything to earn or contribute to our value; it is just part of our design. How we are treated cannot alter our value. *There is nothing anyone can do to us to make us worth less.* What we were created for does not change if we get mistreated, because our value is unchanging.

When we think that our value was determined at the time we were created and our value cannot be added to or diminished, we are better able to put our experiences into perspective. We are able to recognize when we are being celebrated or mistreated, and our value or worth doesn't change with our experience. If we are hurt or traumatized there will be a recovery process, but the event will not define us or become part of our identity. We do not begin to act as though we are worth less than we were before, knowing our value doesn't diminish.

When we encounter someone who is abusive toward us, we should either stop them or remove ourselves from the situation. Having a healthy sense of value keeps us from allowing an abusive person to take charge of us. We recognize abuse when we see it and *we cannot be taken captive because we don't think that way!* The same goes for negative circumstances. We confidently reject captivity's invitation with a simple response, "I don't think so!"

After serving twenty-seven years in prison, Nelson Mandela went on to be president of South Africa. Helen Keller was born blind but lived a life of incredible vision. Corrie Ten Boom lived through the horrors of the Holocaust and went on to use her life to bring healing and freedom to people all around the world by teaching the power of forgiveness. How could these heroes have possibly processed the atrocities committed against them and gone on to live happy, productive lives? They lived on purpose because they understood their value and refused to let circumstances dictate who they were or what they could do. They refused to allow what happened to them to become their identity. They were never hijacked because *they didn't think so.*

The nature of humanity is that we each have the ability to think what we want, whether it is true or not. We can choose to believe that we have intrinsic value, or we can choose to believe that we are not worth anything. When we think we have no value, we look to external experiences or people to validate us. When we are mistreated, we believe that mistreatment is a signal that we are worthless, and we retreat from life, no longer able to function as we were meant to. We naturally conclude that because we don't have worth, we cannot expect to be treated well or accomplish anything. The response that comes from this kind of thinking is an open invitation to hijackers to come in and take charge. It is a common denominator in the lives of people who find themselves hijacked. Captivity begins with a thought. How did captivity happen to me? *I thought so.*

As a child, I allowed how I was treated to determine my worth. Several traumatic, abusive events caused me to form beliefs about myself that diminished my value and led to the beginning of my captivity. My thoughts determined my responses, and my responses eventually became stepping stones into a destructive relationship.

I used to think, *If only that hadn't happened to me, or if only I hadn't been treated that way, everything would have been fine. Today I think, If only I hadn't **thought** that way about what happened to me, everything would have been fine.* I now have a clear understanding that if I had thought differently, I would have responded differently, and not found myself caught in a trap of abuse. I'm not a captive now because *I don't think so.*

What has your response been to negative circumstances in your life? Have circumstances affected how you see yourself? Have they caused you to lose confidence, lower your expectations, and retreat from life? Or have you been able to navigate through them, knowing that they do not change who you are? If you find yourself repeatedly saying, "I'm doing okay under the circumstances," it could be that you have allowed something or someone to hijack your life and that your thinking has opened the door to captivity.

No matter what has taken you captive, you can change your mind. *Because captivity begins with a thought, it can end with a thought.* If you will think differently, you will respond differently. If you respond differently, you will produce a different outcome and a different life from what you have experienced in the past.

Captivity? *I don't think so.*

Chapter 3

RESPONDING TO REJECTION

I was a small-town, prairie-farm girl, and I cherish that upbringing. I enjoyed the ebb and flow of farm life. I loved it in the spring-time when our family would go for a drive to look at the new crops with their tender green shoots poking through the soil and quivering in the breeze. It was the feeling of life. I also loved the smell of harvest in the air as the fall winds came and dried the grain, and the combines headed into the fields. They worked late into the night, their lights shining in the dark as the trucks waited to be filled one more time before calling it a day. It was exhilarating; and when it was all finished, I loved driving the tractor as the cultivator turned the soil over in preparation for another year.

Our family attended church on occasion. I had the privilege of attending Sunday school for a short season before I reached school age. I was mesmerized by the colorful books with the pop-out figures from the Bible stories. I learned songs like "Jesus Loves Me" and "This Little Light of Mine"; they were treasures in my young world.

I started school when I was five years old at the local "little red brick school." It was anything but little to me. It was a big, unfamil-iar world that loomed over me as I entered, making me keenly aware of how small I was. The ceilings were high, the windows were tall, and the polished tile floors smelled of pungent cleaner. The room was more sterile and proper than welcoming. My first-grade teacher was a sharp, middle-aged nun with wire-rimmed glasses and short dark hair. She seldom smiled. She vigilantly enforced a strict code of silence, and shame was her weapon of choice when anyone dared to test the waters. There was no doubt in my mind that she was in charge.

I didn't know the names of the children who sat nearby. There was the tall skinny boy and the short chubby boy who shared a table with me and the cross-eyed girl with the funny laugh who ate her banana peels at lunch time, much to my horror. Our class began each day singing "O Canada" and reciting the "Lord's Prayer." I was eager to learn, and the lessons and books were a world of new experiences that excited me and countered the daunting atmosphere. Receiving my first "Dick and Jane" reader was like receiving the grandest prize I could ever have imagined.

While many things were new, I took most of them in stride. However, a couple of weeks into the school year, something happened that no one had prepared me for. It was a weekly religion class called Catechism. At first, I was thrilled to discover that I was going to learn about God, and I could hardly wait. As the Catechism class began, the teacher rearranged the seating plan a bit, which didn't make any sense to me. I had to move across the room to someone else's seat. Then she instructed the class to stand and say the "Lord's Prayer," just like we had done at the beginning of each day. "Our Father, who art in heaven…," I began earnestly, with my eyes closed, my hands folded and my head bowed. I was very intent on doing a good job of praying. I was jolted from my heartfelt prayer with the blast of her words, "No, not you, you sit down." The sharp command caused me to lose my balance as my eyes flew open and looked up to meet hers. *What do you mean sit down?* I thought frantically to myself. I quickly obeyed, confused and embarrassed, and not understanding what I had done to cause her such displeasure.

The fact was I was a Protestant kid in a Catholic school. Actually, there were four Protestants in the class, three boys and one girl (me!), and seemingly I was the only one who hadn't been informed that the Catholic God wasn't meant for us. No one explained to me why I didn't belong or couldn't participate. Every week when the

Catechism books came out, the four of us were moved to the perimeter of the room and given something else to occupy us while the others studied. I felt guilty for listening, but it was impossible not to. As I did, I heard parts of the gospel. The part about me being a sinner. The part about how bad I was. The part about how much God hated sin. The part about my hopelessness without God. And I heard the remedy, the one for Catholics.

If you were Catholic, you got to pray. You got a Catechism book. You got a rosary. You got to go to church. You got to experience the sacraments. It sounded so glorious! But the message was clear: *I wasn't one of them.* It was somewhat shocking. And while my classmates went through the ordinances of confirmation and first confession, I stood on the outside looking in. It felt a lot like showing up, inappropriately dressed, at a party that I hadn't been invited to. Over time, I got used to it, but some experiences were worse than others. I vividly remember the day in grade two when our class walked along the dusty edge of the highway to the church for confirmation rehearsal. All of the other girls had beautiful white dresses of satin and lace that had been purchased for them in preparation to meet with the priest and have this special moment of connection with their God. I felt so embarrassed and awkward. I didn't belong, but I had to be there, even though it was very painful. I had the same problem they all did—sin. I was the only one without a solution, the only one without a white dress, the only one without a way to make myself *okay* with God.

I was surrounded by Catholic imagery. I wished desperately that I could have a rosary. I stared longingly at the crucifixes on the wall of my best friend's home. At night, in the privacy of my room before I went to sleep, I would practice saying Hail Marys and Our Fathers, since I wasn't allowed to do it with my classmates. I felt like I was sneaking something that wasn't intended for me. But it wasn't being excluded from the group that was the most painful part—it was believing that God had excluded me.

The truth was that my teacher wasn't responsible for my religious training and rightly set me apart from the others. She did not do anything wrong. But the circumstances set me up to wrongly believe that

I had been rejected by God. If I wasn't good enough for God, how could I ever be good enough for anyone? No one knew that in a little girl's heart, a belief had been formed that I wasn't worth much. It was deeply ingrained in me at that tender age that I was deficient and lacking, an outsider with no way to ever really belong. I allowed the situation to define me as different from the rest, as less than acceptable, and naturally I lowered my expectation of what rights I had in the world. I learned to take what was handed out and not ask for more because after all, I was an outsider. I responded to life, not according to the truth, but according to what I thought. By doing so, I invited rejection to become my first hijacker.

Chapter 4

RESPONDING TO ABUSE

With an established sense of low self-worth, I was an easy mark for a predator. My abuser didn't lurk across the street from my school or watch me in a playground. He didn't corner me in a shopping mall. He didn't talk to me online. He came to town wearing a clergyman's collar, introduced himself as the new minister, and invited himself into our home. He was a people-person. He boldly looked my parents in the eyes and shared supper at our kitchen table, and he smiled at me. In fact, he gave me his full attention. He was fun. He brought laughter into my world. He began to play games with me and wrestle with me.

As I described in the first chapter, when you believe that circumstances dictate your value, you welcome abusers into your life through your responses to them. I enjoyed his attention. I felt noticed. I enjoyed a newfound sense of happiness as I forgot about being rejected. No one had ever made me feel the way he did. He brought a smile to my face and joy to my heart. I wasn't good enough for God, but I was special to this man of God. I responded to him with the innocence of a little girl who just wanted to look into someone's face and see in their reflection that she was good.

When he began to put his tongue in my mouth, I did not say a word. Not to him and not to anyone else. I didn't understand why he was doing it, but it didn't seem like that big of a deal at first. As time passed, things progressed, and he began putting his hand in my pants. I didn't like it, and it didn't feel right. But I liked his attention. It made me feel special. I didn't know what would happen if I told. Would I lose his friendship? Would he be angry? I struggled inwardly with my conflicted thoughts. What he was doing didn't seem right, but he was a minister so how could it be wrong? I was too scared to say anything. I wished desperately that he would just stop that part of things.

I do not know how much time elapsed until I made the decision to tell, but I reached a point where my young mind was too overwhelmed to know what to do, and I had to talk to an adult. I sat watching a sitcom with my grandma late one afternoon, shifting back and forth uncomfortably in my chair, wanting to tell and waiting to tell and wondering if I should tell. Finally I couldn't hold it in any longer, and I blurted out the words, "Grandma, do you know what the minister does? He puts his hand in my pants." There. It was out. It wasn't a secret any more. The tremendous weight of the decision I had been struggling with lifted from my shoulders.

Telling on him was the hardest thing I had ever done because, in speaking out, I lost my "friend" and the joy that he brought me with his affection. I never saw him again. I knew my family loved me, but he wasn't family so he didn't have to love me, and that was what had made me feel so special. My temporary sense of value that came from my friendship with him was stripped away, and I was back where I started. However, that wasn't the worst of it.

My mother went to talk to his overseers who instructed him to meet with my parents. I was sent to my aunt's house so the minister could come to our house for the meeting. Afterward, no one commented about what had happened. Although it had been hard to tell, I thought it was the right thing to do, and I expected a sense of having done well to follow. I expected some affirmation from my parents that I had done the right thing, but none came. No one said it was right or wrong or good or bad. It just was. I was left feeling very awkward and uncertain.

The response of the people in authority in the denomination sent me a defining message. Their way of dealing with the minister was to move him to another community. They didn't stop him, they moved him. At first, it was out of sight, out of mind. But I discovered that not only did they move him, they employed him in the summers at the denomination's Bible camp for children and teens as a camp counselor. Now he wasn't just a minister in a church, he was looking after children—lots of children. The unspoken message I received was that I was the problem and that what had happened to me was normal. If it wasn't normal, they would have stopped him and they didn't. I came to the conclusion that I couldn't trust my own feelings. I wondered why I had bothered to tell anyone.

How did I respond to abuse? I blamed myself. I pronounced guilt upon myself. It erupted from my heart, clawed its way into every emotion and every thought, and accused me everywhere I went and in everything I did. My response became part of my identity, a life sentence that crippled my ability to set boundaries or draw lines or identify what was good and what was bad. I determined that just because something feels wrong doesn't mean that it is. I decided that I could never trust my feelings in the same way again.

Abuse became my second hijacker.

Chapter 5

RESPONDING TO TERROR

The third experience that taught me a flawed way of thinking happened in my teens. For reasons I still don't fully understand, conflict arose in a business relationship of my father's and demands began to be made regarding things that belonged to him.

Initially, it seemed that the conflict was just a misunderstanding and that communication would put the conflict to rest, but that was not so. Dissension grew rapidly during several episodes of attempted but fruitless resolution. It didn't seem to matter how hard my dad tried to work things out, or how many times it appeared as if an agreement had been reached, the conflict continued. One issue arose after another, culminating in a land dispute.

As the breach grew wider and threats were made, a dark, ominous cloud settled in over our home and over our lives. People who could have helped refused to get involved and some of them even pointed their fingers at my dad, blaming him for what was happening. I heard all kinds of accusations made against my father. The lies brought incredible pain into an already unbearable situation. My dad was an honest, principled man doing his best to live a good life and provide well for his family. As a result of the ongoing stress, he was crippled by migraine headaches and laid on the couch for days at a time with the back of his calloused hand covering his eyes, trying to block out the agonizing pain.

As I watched my once strong and seemingly invincible father lay there, deep fear took root inside me. There was no way to stop the conflict and nowhere to go for help. Our lives were paralyzed by a situation with no way out, and it seemed that the ordeal would never end. Then the end did come—in an extremely painful way. When I was seventeen years of age, we packed up our belongings and left the only home and life we had ever known. It didn't belong to us anymore. I hated the injustice. I hated feeling helpless. I hated the pain I saw on my parents' faces.

I concluded at that point that life was something that happened to me. It could be good or bad, but the bottom line was—I could do *nothing* about it. There were no choices to make, no solutions to be found, no God to appeal to, no justice to be had, and no way to stop the pain if someone chose to hurt me. It was the finishing touch on a mindset that would set me up for a future of destruction.

Terror had hijacked me, too.

Chapter 6

I THOUGHT SO

I haven't shared my experiences because I feel the need to tell. Those things happened a long time ago and no longer exercise any control over my life. Most people who know me today are unaware that these things happened to me because they no longer define me. I recognize that the people involved have had the opportunity to change in the years that have passed; who they were then is not necessarily who they are now. I have forgiven them and I do not feel that anyone owes me anything. The reason I have shared these experiences is that it is vital for you to understand how I thought about what happened and to recognize that those thoughts formed a mindset that ruled my life.

To sum it up, as a result of what I went through, I thought that how I was treated determined my value. I thought that I could not trust my feelings. I thought that there was nothing I could do when bad things happened to me except wait for them to end. Those thoughts then determined my responses to life as it unfolded. If someone mistreated me, I would feel badly about myself because I thought their treatment demonstrated my lack of value. I would not speak out because I thought I couldn't trust my feelings. Instead of standing up against mistreatment, I just cowered and waited for it to stop. I thought there was nothing I could do about it.

No thought is inherently dangerous in itself. A thought is just a thought. But when a thought is adopted as a rule to live by, it becomes a mindset. I had a wrong mindset. Every time it was necessary to respond to a situation, *my way of thinking ruled my response.* My thoughts dictated what I could and could not do and how I would respond. That's what any wrong mindset does. It begins with a thought that becomes a rule that strips people of their freedom of choice and hijacks them. The mindset becomes an invisible gun held to people's heads that causes them to act in conformity with its rules. The real enemy then, is not a person or situation that wants to take control of us. The real enemy is not something bad that happens to us. *The real enemy is the way of thinking that occupies our minds and forces us to cooperate with that person or situation, giving it control.*

We fail to recognize our own thoughts as an enemy because we simply embrace our thoughts as part of who we are. We are so familiar with our thought patterns that we never consider that they could be a problem. When we observe other people living different lives from us and wonder how that happened or why they got so lucky, we do not imagine that it might be the result of thinking differently. We live under the false conclusion that our problems are caused by people, circumstances, and situations outside of our control. We wait helplessly for those external factors to change so that our lives can improve. Meanwhile, the true hijacker—the way we think—goes undetected and unchallenged. We blame people and we blame circumstances, but the truth is that if we thought differently we would respond differently and not allow ourselves to be taken captive.

Unfortunately, I had allowed myself to be taken captive. I had unknowingly completed the training course in Hijacking 101. I was not conscious that my thoughts had created a set of rules I lived by or that my thoughts dictated that I respond like a victim. They were simply my thoughts and part of my identity. They felt totally familiar to me. I woke up with them in the morning and went to bed with them at night. I never considered that anything could be wrong with them but my thoughts formed a victim mentality that would eventually set me up for destruction.

I didn't look like a victim yet because my outward success as a student masked my victim mindset. I was well-liked, and I was an achiever. I excelled at every challenge put in front of me as far as academics were concerned. My high school years were filled with recognition—best all-round student awards and highest academic achievement awards. If there was an award to earn, I earned it. I rose to the top in all I did. I was the class valedictorian, the year book editor, and a member of the Students' Association. I headed off to college, eager to explore a new world where I assumed my pattern of success would continue. The future looked bright. And it would have been, except for the way I thought. The girl most likely to succeed was really the girl most likely to be destroyed. I was a young woman waiting for a terrorist to hijack my life because I was familiar with terrorists.

Shortly after moving out on my own, I met the man who would become my husband. Over time, he thought for me, spoke for me, and if I made my own decisions, he raged at me. I thought I had no value, and I thought I couldn't trust my feelings, so with open arms and without question, I embraced the next part of life that was *happening* to me. I was an active participant in my own hijacking and didn't even know it. *I became a victim because I thought so.* If I hadn't thought so, I would not have responded the way I did and the outcome would have been different. But the problem was *I did think so.*

That is how most people get hijacked; they think so, just like I did. The way they think, not their circumstances, sets the stage for destruction in their lives. People embrace what they are familiar with, and they respond the way they have been taught. They allow their hijacker to devalue them, define them, and control them. They think their way into captivity. They have a victim mindset, and they are active participants in the hijacking process.

People are quick to name the bad guys in their lives, but it takes two parties to buy in to the same way of thinking that creates dysfunction. The abuser and the victim are just opposite sides of the same coin. I am not saying this to blame, and I am not in any way justifying the behavior of an abuser. But in most situations, if someone came along and took the abuser away, it would only be a temporary solution. *The way abused people think eventually causes them to look for another person to treat them the same way, because they have agreed to and are part of the problem.*

Why does it work this way? It is a law that works, just as surely as the law of gravity works. The Bible tells us, *"For as he thinks in his heart, so is he"* (Proverbs 23:7a NKJV). If people believe that they are victims, then they will respond like victims. In fact, they will attract the very thing they don't want, simply because they believe it about themselves.

Anytime someone is taken captive by a person, an addiction, or a circumstance, it is because he or she developed a mindset that gave jurisdiction over his or her life to their captor. Abuse did not begin for me with an introduction to my future husband, it began with a thought—the same way it does with any kind of captor. Alcoholism doesn't begin with a drink; it begins with a thought. Adultery doesn't begin with a kiss; it begins with a thought. Divorce doesn't begin with an argument; it begins with a thought. Poverty doesn't begin with an unpaid bill; it begins with a thought. A thought becomes a rule that becomes a mindset. The mindset robs people of their freedom, and they no longer have control of their lives.

Mindsets not only develop from a person's experiences, they are also passed down in families. The same thinking that creates captivity in a parent's life is naturally taught to the children. *The parents think so and teach their children to think so, and on it goes.* Abuse, alcoholism, sickness, poverty, and other hijackers plague families for generations because each generation thinks the way the previous one did. Mindsets explain why a woman can go from one abusive relationship to another, why an addict can exchange one addiction for another, or why people repeatedly appear to be magnets for a certain kind of trouble. The players in their lives come and go but their thinking remains the same. The same kind of things will continue to happen until someone in the family realizes that he or she has an option and decides, *"I don't think so."* With a single thought the person can respond differently, overthrow the rule of the hijacker, and walk away free.

When I realized that I was living what I thought, I was set free. The mindset that had bound me for years was broken. If my thoughts were the problem, I could change them. That was exciting, because I had spent years believing that I was powerless to change anything. For the first time ever, I felt a sense of control over my own life. I was no longer a prisoner, and I never would be again.

How did I overcome abuse? The first step was that *I didn't think so anymore.*

Chapter 7

PAIN IS A SIGNAL

Abuse is generally a gradual process. There is an eroding away of people's worth by the words spoken to them, accusations made against them, blame laid on them, and things done to them. It may be constant or it may be sporadic, with periods of normalcy in between. People live in a constant state of anxiety wondering when the rug is going to be pulled out from under them and abuse inflicted upon them once more.

The symptoms that begin to manifest in an abused person's life can include withdrawal, lethargy, loneliness, and loss of motivation. Instead of enjoying life, the person becomes defensive and begins to hide his or her true feelings in an attempt to avoid being abused again. The person is probably not identifying the way he or she is being treated as abuse, but are acutely aware of the pain felt. Avoiding pain becomes the person's primary motivation and he or she moves into a world of isolation where he or she can cope by negotiating, keeping a low profile, and even ignoring the abuse. The person lowers expectations because that eases the pain a little.

The effects intensify over time because hijackers are never satisfied. An abuser is never satisfied. Fear is never satisfied. Addiction is never satisfied. Disease is never satisfied. Poverty is never satisfied. They will always demand more. For that reason, abuse almost always escalates. When the pain becomes too much to bear, victims look for a way of escape but seldom find one because they believe that they themselves are the problem, or they believe that there is nothing they can do about it.

The presence of pain is intended to cause us to change our behavior. Pain is a signal, not an emotion. It is a God-given response built into our DNA that is meant to protect us. When I was five years old, I was helping Grandma bake sweet biscuits. I was sitting on the kitchen counter next to the stove. In spite of her adamant warning, I leaned over and put the palm of my small hand down on a red hot burner. The message of the searing pain registered instantly, and I yanked my hand back. My entire palm blistered, but because I responded immediately to the pain, the damage was controlled.

Abused people wrongly think that pain is a sign that something is wrong with them. As a result, they feel pain and do nothing. They treat it like a false alarm and ignore its signal. The built-in protection system that is meant to direct them away from abuse fails.

When nothing was done to stop the man who molested me as a child, I stopped trusting my feelings. I blamed myself and thought that my feelings were invalid. From my perspective, the pain did not signal abuse or danger; it signaled that something was wrong with me. I continued to think the same way into adulthood. In my marriage, it didn't matter how much pain I felt, I always thought it was my fault that I was being treated that way. I remember how painfully lonely my wedding day was as I married a man who was not speaking to me because of an argument we had the night before. I remember how painfully lonely I felt on the day my son was born. I remember many painful experiences and hours of tears over meaningless arguments and cutting accusations. There was pain in the good times and pain in the bad times. That pain should have been a signal to me to do something, but I did not understand it. I blamed myself for the pain rather than identifying that something needed to change. To use the analogy of the stove, instead of removing my hand, I blamed myself for putting my hand there in the first place and left it there to keep burning. Pain kept me critically aware of how bad I was. We can't make pain go away by blaming ourselves for it. We can say we were stupid or that we did something wrong, but the pain will only continue, because it is a signal to us to change. The sooner we pay attention, the sooner the pain will stop.

I went through a long season of trying to fix everything that could possibly be wrong with me; I was certain that every time I felt pain, I was the problem. I tried to identify what provoked the anger and mistreatment so that I could avoid that behavior, but I could never figure it out. There did not seem to be a pattern. I questioned my motives unceasingly because of the constant accusations made toward me. I read books. I looked for answers, mostly in secret because I felt so badly about myself. In spite of these efforts, the pain did not stop. It seemed to be a life sentence with no possibility of parole.

In my continued quest to overcome my perceived inadequacies, I signed up for a weekly self-esteem course offered in our city. Each week I listened to other women share their stories. Although I never said a word, I wept through nearly every session as their stories gave me permission to acknowledge the pain I was feeling. My heart found solace in knowing that at least I was not alone. They, too, were sentenced to lives of pain. A few weeks passed and as I sat with tears streaming silently down my face again, one of the women in the group looked me in the eyes and said, "Dogs get treated better than you do." Her words sliced through my twisted thinking. What I heard her say was, "How you are being treated is not normal." She voiced pain's signal—"Do something! Take your hand off the burner!" It was a defining moment as I realized that I was not hurting because of my faults or failures; I was hurting because of the way I was being treated. I finally understood that the pain I felt was a signal to change.

Pain is always a signal. But when people interpret it through a mindset, a set of rules that they have to live by, it usually gets misinterpreted. It is seen as an emotion or consequence that has to be endured and its warning goes unheeded. I have often heard people use the expression, "He hasn't hit bottom yet," when talking about someone who is living in a destructive manner. The implication is that the person has not yet felt enough pain to provoke him to change his behavior. I believe the problem is seldom a lack of pain. I think that more often the problem is that people see pain as an emotion to be endured rather than a signal to change course, and they don't do anything about it because they don't know they should.

No matter how much pain there is, until victims determine for themselves that what is happening in their lives isn't normal, they will remain victims of whatever has hijacked them. It is not enough for someone else to see their problem; they have to see it for themselves. That's the way it was for me. I had totally given up my identity and had become a walking shell of a person. I spent my days going through the motions and doing my best to care for my son. My hope, my passion, and my energy were gone.

I remember one day when I invited an acquaintance over for coffee in an attempt to find some enjoyment in life. Although my house was clean, my young son had smeared a snack all over the living room coffee table. As I sat visiting with my guest, I kept thinking to myself, "I need to wipe the table," but I could not summon the strength to actually do it. I found it difficult to even carry on a normal conversation with someone because I did not have the emotional energy and focus required to connect. I poured what little strength I did have into becoming whatever I needed to be on any particular day, in order to survive. It did not matter how lonely or desperate I felt, I wasn't able to determine for myself that things weren't normal. Why? Because my thoughts kept vigilant guard over my responses, and I just kept doing the same things over and over again.

When the woman at the self-esteem class verbalized what I had been denying for so long, she confronted me with truth. She challenged my mindset—the way of thinking that ruled my life and demanded a victim response to abuse. It took the voice of a total stranger to help me see the pain in a different way. I listened to her words over and over again in my head, absorbing what she had said. The pain was a signal that there was a problem, not that I was the problem. For the first time I was able to evaluate what the pain really meant, and heed its signal. I recognized that how I was being treated was not normal, and the cords that had bound me for so long began to loosen their hold. By changing my thinking I was freeing myself. No one was rescuing me; in fact no one could. *I was freeing myself by changing my mind.*

There was no outward sign of change, but on the inside I was different. On the inside, I began to call things as they really were. I began to let go of the thoughts that had been so deeply entrenched in my life and explore new ones. I stopped blaming myself. I stopped thinking that I was the problem. I stopped thinking that there was nothing I could do.

As time passed and I saw my life from this new perspective, I reached a point when I knew without a doubt that I wouldn't survive in my marriage. Although I couldn't see any way out, I knew I couldn't go on the same way anymore. Heeding pain's signal, I left my marriage when I was twenty-seven years of age, with my young son in my arms. I remember driving down the highway, with no idea of where to go or what to do, and no idea what future lay ahead of me. In desperation, I cried out to the God who I thought had rejected me as a child. "God, I don't know if there's any way out of this alive, and I know I don't deserve anything from You, but I have this innocent child who I don't know how to protect...for his sake, would You help me?"

More important than the fact that I physically removed myself from the circumstances that day was the fact that in that moment I confronted the foundation of my faulty belief system. Most of my life I had thought God had rejected me, but that day I dared to believe that *perhaps* His mercy was greater than my failure.

It was a whole new way of thinking.

Chapter 8

WHEN TROUBLE TAKES CONTROL

A buse is not the only terrorist that hijacks people's lives. When people experience trouble, they should navigate their way through the trouble and come out on the other side. People lose their jobs and go through difficult financial seasons, but eventually they should get another job and recover. Other people might have accidents that injure their bodies, but eventually as the injuries are treated and time passes, life should return to normal. In other words, we fall down, but we are meant to get back up again.

When trouble begins to dictate what a person can and cannot do for an extended period of time, a hijacking is in progress. When a small financial problem becomes a credit card debt that eventually leaves a person unable to afford anything, a hijacking has taken place. When a simple glass of wine with dinner becomes something a person cannot live without, a hijacking has taken place. When a routine medical test to see why someone isn't feeling well becomes a life full of symptoms that controls a person's every move, a hijacking has taken place. When a small worry becomes a crippling phobia, a hijacking has taken place. It does not matter what the hijacker's name is, when a person believes the hijacker's lies, the person exchanges freedom for the bondage of trying to meet the hijacker's unending and impossible demands.

The presence of a hijacker is revealed by the fact that people who have been taken hostage are unable to live their lives without asking the hijacker for permission. Generally, when they do ask, permission will be denied. When opportunity knocks, a hostage will almost always decline the invitation, citing reasons such as, "I can't because I'm broke," or "I'm sick," or "I'm depressed." The victim has moved beyond an experience and has actually taken on the identity of the hijacker. The excuses reveal what it is that has taken the person captive and is ruling over his or her life.

What has hijacked or defined your life? Is it sickness or fear? Poverty or addiction? Workaholism or perfectionism? Grief or depression? Perhaps you don't even know whether or not you've been hijacked; you just know you are not living a quality life.

Here is a test you can take to see if your life has been hijacked. Imagine that a good friend invites you to go on a week's vacation six months from now, to a place that you would really enjoy visiting. Your friend describes how you will spend your time there and it includes all of the things that you love to do. What would your response be? Would you wholeheartedly accept the invitation? Or would you say that even though you would love to, there are several reasons why you can't? There genuinely could be some reasons for you to say no, such as not being able to get the time off from work or not having enough resources. But what would your response be if you were given time and finances?

If you chose not to go, then something has likely hijacked your life and you bow down to it no matter what you want or what opportunity comes your way. You will decline most invitations and opportunities by describing what you have allowed to hijack you and by listing its reasons for not letting you go. If it is finances, then you will describe your financial situation in detail and explain how the vacation is not possible. If it is sickness, then you will describe the sickness in detail and explain how it is not possible. If it is work, then you will describe all of the work you have to do and explain how it is not possible for you to go. The interesting thing is that all of your reasons for saying no will sound completely legitimate to you. They will make sense. But if time can't change the circumstances, then you are not free.

If it is fear or an addiction that has hijacked you, then you probably would not offer those things as excuses to your friend because you wouldn't want your friend to know, but you will make up some other excuse in its place. Regular, repeated dishonesty is another indicator that you are the victim of some controlling power in your life.

The process works the same in any of these situations as it does with someone who is hijacked by abuse. The trouble itself is not the hijacker; the hijacker is the mindset with which the trouble is embraced. Trouble should never take control of your life. If you encounter trouble, you must deal with it, but you do not have to let it take over. Refuse to give it control. Refuse to ask its permission about what you can and cannot do. Do not identify with it! It will have an end if you approach it with the right mindset.

I watched a lovely young woman, a cherished wife and mother, fight a heroic battle with cancer. Although the cancer eventually took her life, it never took her soul. She never became its victim. She never identified herself with it, even though she had to live with its effects. How do I know that? She never stopped loving, giving, or being who she was, even though she had to deal with the experience of cancer. In contrast, I've met people with non life-threatening illnesses who have totally given themselves over to their disease and let it define them. Something is happening beyond the physical symptoms they are experiencing. They begin to introduce themselves in terms of their sickness, make life choices based on their sickness, and identify themselves with their sickness. It is not meant to be that way. Their minds have been hijacked.

Do not be alarmed if you are recognizing that something has hijacked your life. The good news is that you do not have to stay that way! You do not have to remain a victim. Your circumstances or experiences do not have to define you. You can be free if you will change your mind. Every time trouble makes a move to take control of your life, respond with a confident, "I don't think so."

Chapter 9

UNCOVERING THE LIES

The lies we live by create a system of thought that forms the foundation of captivity and abuse. In fact, this is how sin entered the world. I have shared with you the things that happened in my formative years that set me up for destruction, and how the lies I believed as a result of those events gave abuse power over me.

When the authorities failed to stop the minister who molested me, I believed the lies that I was the problem and that my feelings could not be trusted. The truth is that the authorities were cowards—grown men unwilling to deal with the responsibility they had toward me and other unsuspecting children. My feelings that the minister's behavior was wrong were completely accurate. And when our family was in conflict, I believed the lie that there was no way to resolve it and nowhere to turn for help. The truth is that God was with me the whole time.

But the greatest lie of all, the one most damaging to my life, was the lie that I first believed during grade one Catechism—the lie that I was separated from God. I believed there was no place for me in His world. I clearly understood that I was a sinner and so was everyone else. I could grasp that. (See Romans 3:23.) But along with that truth was the lie that there was no remedy for my sin, no way to bridge the gap between God and me. There was no hope of ever being "right" with God. I had started school singing "Jesus Loves

Me," but I soon developed a new picture of Him in my mind. He became an angry God who sat aloof on His throne, watching over people for one thing only—to see when they sinned so He could punish them. I saw Him as a God of judgment and wrath, and I feared Him more than anything. There was no way to be right with Him and no way to appease Him. It was a lie I lived by throughout my childhood.

That lie caused me to become the Cinderella of my own world. I was allowed to be in the family; I was allowed to work with and serve the family; but when the ball came, I knew there would never be an invitation with my name on it. I would never be celebrated because the party would never be for me and the prince would never come for me. When you can't expect a prince, you will accept anyone who comes along, because at least then you don't have to be alone. In believing that lie, I accepted a lot of things that came along, subjecting myself to pain and abuse.

Years later, when I left my marriage, I did not know what to do or where to go. In my desperation, I chose to cry out to God although I still had the same false picture of Him in my mind. I still believed I was disgraceful in His sight, but I dared to ask for help for the sake of my young child. I was about to discover that God was not angry with me; nor did He want to punish me. I was about to be introduced to the God who loved me and had a plan for my life.

I went to stay with my parents who lived in a small town. Word about the desperate situation I was in quickly spread around the community and a pastor in the town heard the news. He did not know me or my family so there was no reason for him to reach out to a complete stranger, and yet he did. Ignoring the awkwardness that comes from approaching someone's home uninvited, he chose to knock on our door, introduce himself, and ask if there was anything he could do to help. He spent some time praying with my family and invited us to church. I am so thankful that he did.

When Sunday came, I went. I had been to church before but this was different. *For the first time, I heard what was being said instead of what I thought was being said.* I could actually hear God's love for me in the words that were being preached. I felt hopeful that God was with me instead of against me. The words brought life to my soul. The people I met there welcomed me, and church quickly became the only place in my chaotic world where I felt safe. For a little while, I felt calm. For a little while, I felt safe. For a little while, I forgot what was waiting for me outside the church doors. As the service would draw to a close, suddenly I would be gripped with fear knowing I had to leave and couldn't come back again for another week. Church was the only refuge from the storm of my life.

A few short weeks after I prayed my first desperate prayer asking God to have mercy on me and help me for the sake of my child, I made another bold move. I was listening to a Christian radio program one afternoon when an opportunity was given to receive Christ. I knew without a doubt that was what I wanted to do. In response to the invitation, I knelt on the living room floor, bowed my head, and said a prayer that went something like this: "God, I've sinned. Today, I repent and turn from my sins, and I ask You to forgive me. I invite Jesus to come into my heart and be the Lord of my life."

God answered that prayer. He was not the angry, raging God I had expected Him to be. He was not watching, scrutinizing, or judging me. He did not respond to me with a list of my mistakes or failures. He did not point a finger at me or accuse me. He welcomed me into relationship with Him, flooding my heart with peace.

I found out that I had believed lies about God my entire life. The words I had been living by were untrue. God did not hate me; He loved me. What He hated was sin because sin hurts people. He had dealt with my sin and everyone else's by sending Jesus to die on the cross in our place. He took the penalty for the punishment we deserve because He loves us. The cross was the ultimate act of love that brought me into relationship with God *my* Father. I discovered what I had failed to hear in Catechism—the cross was for everyone. The Amplified version of John 3:16 tells us, *"For God so greatly loved the world and dearly prized the world that He [even] gave up His only begotten (unique) Son, so that whoever believes in (trusts in, clings to, relies on) Him shall not perish (come to destruction, be lost) but have eternal (everlasting) life."* The power of the lie that said there was no way to bridge the gap between God and me was broken. God's Word, the truth, set me free.

If you have lived for a long time with abuse, addiction, sickness, or any other hijacker, it will have tangled you in its web of lies. Each one of those lies separates you from God. You must uncover them and establish the truth in their place just as I did.

How do you do that? How do you find your way to the truth? You must understand how you were deceived in the first place. The Bible tells us that before sin entered the world, Adam and Eve lived naked (transparent, fully known) in the presence of God without any consciousness of sin. *Sin is simply anything that separates us from God.* Adam and Eve had been created according to God's design, in His image, and they were good. They had no self-image because they had never imagined themselves apart from God. When they thought about themselves, they thought about God; and He was good, so they had to be good too. That is how God intended it.

It never occurred to Adam and Eve that there could be anything deficient about them. It never occurred to them to be afraid of anything. They had never experienced a single thought of rejection, guilt, or isolation. Eve never asked Adam, "Do I look fat in this outfit?" and she never told him, "I have nothing to wear for dinner tonight!" She never thought about an extreme makeover. The reason was because, in her mind, she had no identity separate from God. She had no self-concept! Adam never wondered if he was handsome enough or if he made enough money. He never worried whether or not Eve might leave him. And neither of them ever said, "I really blew it today. I feel so guilty!" They had no sin consciousness.

It was a lie that caused Adam and Eve to sin. Genesis 3:5 tells how the serpent, God's enemy, implied that they were lacking something, and if they just ate from God's forbidden tree of the knowledge of good and evil, then they wouldn't be lacking anymore. In fact, he told them they would become like God. The truth was they were already like God. When Adam and Eve believed the serpent's lie and then acted on it by taking from the tree, their belief system was shattered. That single lie exploded into a whole new system of thought, and Adam and Eve saw themselves differently from the way they had before. In their minds they went from being like God or inseparable from Him, to being separated from Him. Sin had entered the world.

Genesis 3 goes on to describe what happened next. As usual, God came to spend time with Adam and Eve in the cool of the day. But where were they? They were hiding and cowering. God called to Adam and asked him where he was. Adam responded, "I heard Your voice in the garden and I was afraid because I was naked, and I hid myself." Afraid? Since when? Naked? Since when? Hiding? Since when? They were afraid, naked, and hiding because they believed the lie that the enemy told them. A lie separated them from God and a self-image apart from God developed in their minds. They had let their sin define them and devalue them. They went from being God-conscious to self-conscious and concluded they were deficient. Instead of having a relationship with God, they believed that He was a master to cower from.

God's response to Adam's explanation was a question: "Who told you that you were naked?" He was not asking as an angry out-of-control parent would, demanding to know, "Who did this?" or "How could you have done this?" Those questions are a misconception believed by some. No, God's question reveals the broken heart of a loving Father who recognized that His children allowed something to define them other than Him. He knew that they had been separated from Him. He knew that they believed a lie. In grief, He was asking His beloved, "Who told you that you were naked?"

If you were to hear God's voice speaking to you today, you might hear Him asking the same question. It might sound like this: "Who told you that you were worthless? Who told you that you deserved to be abused? Who told you that you were deficient? Who told you that you were unlovable? Who told you that you were to blame? Who told you such a lie?"

Any lie we believe will not only change our sense of value, it will also strip us of our God-given identity and separate us from

Him in our minds. The Bible tells us in Isaiah 59:2 that *"There's nothing wrong with God; the wrong is in you. Your wrongheaded lives caused the split between you and God..."* (MSG). Once our identity has been robbed, we will live under the rule of the one who covered us with the lie. Even if we have some sense of God, we no longer think we are like Him because we have allowed the lie to separate us from Him. We become sin-conscious and we make lists of things we do that we believe will separate us from God. That's not really surprising; after all, the Ten Commandments are a list of things we should not do. But sin doesn't originate in an action; sin originates in our thoughts when we believe a lie that separates us in our minds from God. The Bible tells us that, *"nothing can ever separate us from God's love. Neither death nor life, neither angels nor demons, neither our fears for today nor our worries about tomorrow—not even the powers of hell can separate us from God's love"* (Romans 8:38).

If you are living in abuse or some other kind of captivity, then at some point you have believed something about yourself that was a lie. One lie became many lies that tangled your thinking until you no longer knew what to believe. As you recognize those lies, instead of blaming yourself, realize that you have an enemy who pointed out some deficiency or inadequacy and hijacked your life.

God's righteous anger toward the enemy who lied to Eve and separated all of humanity from Him is the same righteous anger toward the enemy who lied to you. God's anger was expressed in the most passionate display of love anyone could ever have imagined. He sent His only Son Jesus to earth to die for us. That act of love dealt with the sin or separation from God that we were born with. Second Corinthians 5:21 tells us that *"God made him who had no sin to be sin for us, so that in him we might become the righteousness of God"* (NIV). We were separated from God; Jesus was in perfect relationship with God. Jesus exchanged places with us. Our sin demanded judgment, and He took our place, in essence saying, "Take me instead; I'll pay the penalty." Jesus became sin and God turned His back on sin. We hear the cost of that choice when Jesus cries out on the cross, *"...My God, my God, why have you forsaken Me [deserting Me and leaving Me helpless and abandoned]?"* (Mark 15:34

AMP). Jesus was forsaken as He suffered the wrath that we deserved. He took our place and gave us His. An exchange took place; and in that moment, we were made righteous and given right standing with God.

As Jesus died in our place, He overcame every enemy humankind would ever know, destroying the power of sin that had mastered us. Three days later, Jesus rose from the dead, restoring to us our true identities as sons and daughters of God.

God didn't just ask, "Who did this?" He stopped the hijacking. He took responsibility for it and paid the full ransom so that we would not have to live under abuse, fear, poverty, addiction, or depression ever again. If we will turn our eyes from ourselves to the cross of Christ, if we will see the life that was given for us, then no one will ever be able to hijack us again with a lie. We do that by believing the truth. Sin hijacked humankind when Adam and Eve believed a lie. Humankind has victory over sin when we believe the truth.

Romans 10:8-10 says,

> "...The word that saves is right here, as near as the tongue in your mouth, as close as the heart in your chest. It's the word of faith that welcomes God to go to work and set things right for us. This is the core of our preaching. Say the welcoming word to God—'Jesus is my Master'—embracing, body and soul, God's work of doing in us what he did in raising Jesus from the dead. That's it. You're not 'doing' anything; you're simply calling out to God, trusting him to do it for you. That's salvation. With your whole being you embrace God setting things right, and then you say it, right out loud: 'God has set everything right between him and me!'" (MSG).

Chapter 10

DEFEATING DISAPPOINTMENT

I can still remember that day in grade two as if it were yesterday. It was Catechism class and we were walking down the dusty edge of the highway to go to the church. Everyone was preparing for their confirmation in the Catholic Church. Well, everyone except me, because I was Protestant. All of the girls had beautiful white dresses for the occasion. Except me. It was difficult being the only one not wearing a white dress. I had been excluded from a special event that everyone else had been invited to attend. The emotions I felt were twofold. First of all there was the pain of not wearing a beautiful white dress. Second, there was embarrassment that everyone knew there was no dress for me. I felt embarrassed and vulnerable. If I could have stayed behind, alone in the classroom, it would have been easier, but I had to walk with the rest of the class. There was nowhere to take cover. All I could do was pretend it did not matter.

There are times when I still wrestle with those same kinds of feelings. In defeating the hijackers in your life, there is still the reality that some circumstances or events take place that we cannot control. They do not need to defeat us, because we always have control over our response to them, but sometimes we go through circumstances where there is no white dress for us. We go through circumstances or situations that we are powerless to change. The pain and embarrassment are worse when no one around us seems to be experiencing the same problem. Just like not having a white dress, it is painful when we are unable to attain something we want and at the same time, it is embarrassing when everyone around us seems to have it.

The most painful issue in my life was losing custody of my son. When he was four years of age, the courts awarded full custody of him to his father. It was devastating. When I awoke the morning after he was taken from me, the pain was so bad that I could barely breathe. I didn't know how I would survive the next ten minutes, much less think about getting on with my life. My heart was broken. There was nothing I wanted more than to have my son returned to me. It felt unbearable to be separated from him. It didn't seem to matter what I did, I was powerless to do anything to change the situation. It hurt being apart from him. It hurt not knowing if he was doing okay or not. It was awful when he would beg me not to leave him, and I would have to peel myself away from him, turn my back and walk away. Every single day I woke up feeling as though I had been punched in the stomach, as I remembered once again that he was gone.

There were seasons when the pain was less intense than others, but the pain was particularly bad during holidays. Holidays were always a cruel reminder that another season or another year had passed and nothing had changed. God had not answered my prayers and my heart still hurt. When there was no holiday, I could bury my nose in work and take the edge off of the pain, but invariably the calendar would turn and the reminders would come.

Sometimes I would meet other people who were in a similar situation, who didn't have their children living with them. I would watch things change for them seemingly effortlessly. The other parent would call and say they were giving them their child. Or they would pray a single prayer and the next thing they knew, their child was back living with them. While I was happy for them, at times I would think to myself, *They are not even very good parents. Why is God giving them their children back but ignoring my cry?*

This was my particular point of vulnerability. In grade two, everyone could have a white dress—except me. Now I was grown up and everyone could have their children—except me. Your white dress story might be completely different. Perhaps you are one of those couples who want nothing more than to have a baby, but you can't conceive. You watch as the years pass and all of your friends have babies, but it doesn't happen for you. Or maybe you are even told you will never have children. Some of your friends get pregnant and wish they weren't, and you carry untold pain around in your heart as you hear them complain. It wouldn't hurt so much if you weren't surrounded by people who have what you are powerless to get.

It may not be a baby for you. It could be marriage. Perhaps you have watched all of your friends fall in love with the man or woman of their dreams, but you are still alone. You wonder what they know that you don't; and as the years go by and they celebrate anniversaries, you question whether there will ever be anyone for you. You try to act as though you are fine with being single, and you may be content, but there are still the awkward situations where you are the only single and the conversation is centered on marriage and children and family. You are in the family, but excluded from the party. I never dreamed that I would be single for a long time. I never dreamed that I wouldn't have more children. I never dreamed that I wouldn't raise the child I did have.

Perhaps you have not been able to break through in your career or your business. Perhaps you have done the things your peers have done and yet the deals have not materialized, the doors have not opened, the increase has not come. Maybe you have watched your friends move up in the world, but try as you might you still barely get by. It is tough. And it is worse when you cannot hide it.

Or perhaps you have struggled with some sort of sickness or disease and have not received your healing. You have watched other people get healed, you may have even prayed for other people and have seen them healed—yet your symptoms don't go away. It is humiliating when you have to reveal to everyone around you that you are still sick.

How do you deal with this pain? How do you face what is out of your control without it hijacking you? How do you keep from becoming a victim?

The first thing you must do is realize that no matter what you are going through, God is faithful. There are some things that we will never understand or have answers for until we meet God face to face in eternity. But you can know that God is faithful to you in the midst of every painful circumstance that you are unable to change. I can look back on my life and the things I have had to go through and remember the pain of it all, and yet I can tell you this—God has been faithful. He has never left me even for a moment. He has been my strength in weakness, my comfort in pain, and my healing in brokenness. People hurt me and let me down, but God was always faithful. It's not possible for Him to be anything else. Isaiah 61:3 says that God *"...will give a crown of beauty for ashes, a joyous blessing instead of mourning, festive praise instead of despair...."*

Second, you have to be willing to let God answer your prayers in whatever manner He deems best. After I lost custody of my son, I never wanted to set foot in a courtroom again or have a judge rule over my life again; I was quite adamant that God would never make me do that. Nearly ten years later, when my son turned fourteen and determined for himself that he wanted to live with me, the only way for that to happen was in a courtroom. Although I did not want to go back there, it was the way that God brought the answer to my years of prayers. It was not the way I wanted it to happen, but today I am thankful that God used another judge in another courtroom to reverse what had happened.

I have friends who have struggled for years with the pain of infertility. I have prayed with them and encouraged them and have been there for them as they walked the path that they seemed unable to change. Sometimes there were reasons for the infertility and sometimes it was unexplained. The report from the fertility clinic would come back—no known cause. The more time that passed and the more babies their friends had, the more painful life became. There is no magic formula. For one friend, the answer came through the help of a fertility clinic. For another, the answer came with a phone call from a friend who said, "I know a girl who is pregnant and doesn't want to keep her baby." For another, the answer came after eight years of waiting and then a simple prayer, a medical procedure, and a positive pregnancy test. There were no bad answers to those prayers. Even when we do not get the answer we hoped for, I believe that God's answer is enough. Second Corinthians 12:9 says, *"and then he told me, My grace is enough; it's all you need. My strength comes into its own in your weakness. Once I heard that, I was glad to let it happen. I quit focusing on the handicap and began appreciating the gift. It was a case of Christ's strength moving in on my weakness"* (MSG).

Third, you have to discover God's will for yourself. In situations where there are no explanations why you are not getting what you are believing for, and no tangible ways to change the situation, it is not enough to know what other people think about it. Sometimes the first place we look to for guidance is the opinions of others. We want someone to reassure us that God will hear us and that our prayers will be answered. We want someone to prophesy to us that everything is going to be all right. Even when that does happen, when people are willing to share their perspective or their opinion, we can still be left uncertain and hurting.

For years I went through a never-ending cycle of getting my hopes up, waiting, and then realizing nothing had changed. The pain of the disappointment would cause me to feel numb for a while in order to cope with it. Then something else would raise my faith and I would begin to believe again. Then time would pass and nothing would happen. Again, I would become numb. Hope. Disappointment. Numbness. Hope. Disappointment. Numbness. This cycle went on for years. I didn't know how to resolve it, so I just kept on going. It was painful and it was embarrassing because all around me people had their families together; and no matter how hard I tried, nothing changed.

One day when things were not going well for my son, I said to a trusted mentor, "He really needs to be back with me now." She responded by saying, "Well, I don't know what God's will is, but I'll pray." She did not mean for her words to shock me, but they did. I thought to myself, *If you don't know what God's will is, then who does?* She was one of the most spiritual people I knew. Suddenly my confidence in all of the prayers I had been praying asking God to return my son to me was gone. It was like the rug had been pulled out from underneath me. I did not know what I should believe anymore. I wondered if I had been praying incorrectly all along and asking God for something that was contrary to His will.

I could not deal with that uncertainty anymore. I had hoped and waited for too long. I couldn't deal with the pain of another disappointment. I did not have the strength to get my hopes up one more time, only to see them dashed again. I needed to know where God stood on the matter. No one else's opinion was going to help me. Alone with God, I stated my case. "God, I don't know what Your will is, but I want to. I want my son to return to me. If there is any reason in Your Word why that should not happen, then You show me, and I will accept that and stop asking You for it to happen. I won't understand it, but I will choose to trust You."

For the next two weeks, every time I opened my Bible to read God's Word, I also opened my heart to hear whatever God wanted to speak to me. I was waiting for Him to show me any reason my prayer was wrong. I was giving Him the opportunity to say no to me. At the end of those two weeks, I closed my Bible and I knew it was over. God had not shown me anything, and I knew that I was praying the right prayer. Although nothing had changed in the natural, that day things changed in my heart. I didn't know how it would happen or when it would happen, and I knew there was nothing I could do to make it happen, but I knew my son was coming back to live with me. It was done, and I never doubted again. The cycle was broken and disappointment was defeated. There was no more embarrassment because I knew in my heart my prayer had been answered. Five months later, as I was driving home after saying another painful good-bye to my son as I put him on a plane to fly back to his father's home, my cell phone rang. As I said hello, I heard my son's voice on the other end saying, "Mom, I got off the plane." What he was really saying was that he was coming home. It was the best news ever. But it had happened five months earlier when I decided in my heart that disappointment would not rule over me any longer.

No matter what the area of life is where you struggle with the pain and disappointment of unanswered prayer, do not lose hope. God will be faithful to you. He has answers prepared for you that you know nothing of. Stay close to Him and let your life be defined by what He says in His Word about you, not by what you see in the circumstances around you. I woke up every day for nearly ten years feeling like I had been punched in the stomach because my son was gone. Today, I don't remember. Most days I forget that it even happened and I have to think really hard to remember what it felt like.

Something that had the potential power to destroy my life is today only a distant memory. I refused to let it define me; and in doing so, I defeated disappointment. Another friend who as a young mom went through a serious battle with cancer, had a similar experience. Today she is cancer free. She recently told me, "Unless I'm ministering to someone, I forget that I even had cancer. It doesn't define me." My friends who anguished over their barrenness don't remember all the tears they cried waiting for a child. Find out what God's Word says about your situation, and refuse to let disappointment define your life. God will have the final Word.

Isaiah 35:1-10 says,

"The wilderness and the wasteland shall be glad for them, and the desert shall rejoice and blossom as the rose; it shall blossom abundantly and rejoice, even with joy and singing. The glory of Lebanon shall be given to it, the excellence of Carmel and Sharon. They shall see the glory of the Lord, the excellency of our God. Strengthen the weak hands, and make firm the feeble knees. Say to those who are fearful-hearted, "Be strong, do not fear! Behold, your God will come with vengeance, with the recompense of God; He will come and save you." Then the eyes of the blind shall be opened, and the ears of the deaf shall be unstopped. Then the lame shall leap like a deer, and the tongue of the dumb sing. For waters shall burst forth in the wilderness, and streams in the desert. The parched ground shall become a pool, and the thirsty land springs of water; in the habitation of jackals, where each lay, there shall be grass with reeds and rushes. A highway shall be there, and a road, and it shall be

called the Highway of Holiness. The unclean shall not pass over it, but it shall be for others. Whoever walks the road, although a fool, shall not go astray. No lion shall be there, nor shall any ravenous beast go up on it; it shall not be found there. But the redeemed shall walk there, and the ransomed of the Lord shall return, and come to Zion with singing, with everlasting joy on their heads. They shall obtain joy and gladness, and sorrow and sighing shall flee away" (NKJV).

Chapter 11

UNDERSTANDING A VICTIM MENTALITY

One fall, a friend gave me a complimentary registration to attend a weekend workshop that I thought would be about life skills. Some of my other friends were going, and I was excited to have been invited. The instructor was a beautiful, gentle woman and very sincere in her desire to help women live better lives. She was firm but very understanding; and by midway through the second day, I was thoroughly enjoying her teaching.

In the afternoon session, she began describing how some people feel about life. My heart leapt as I heard her say things like, "Bad things have happened to you. You feel like you have been a target for mistreatment. Things never seem to go your way, and day after day you wonder what might happen next." It was as if she was reading my mind. She described my inner world perfectly. I was excited to have someone understand me so well. I thought to myself, *This is going to be fantastic. She knows exactly how I feel. She is going to be able to help me with this pain.* But I was in for a surprise.

When it was time for her to sympathize with me, or say how terrible the things were that had happened to me; when it was time for her to recognize the injustice and accuse those who had hurt me— she didn't. She began to talk instead about a way of thinking. I was bewildered, wondering what way of thinking she meant. How could she equate the bad things that had happened to me with a way of thinking? What did a way of thinking have to do with it? And did she mean there were other ways of thinking if it was "a" way of thinking? My mind raced as I tried to process it. Did this mean that not everyone thought the way I did? Did it mean I wasn't thinking right? And if there was another way for me to think, what was it?

She seemed to be saying that life wasn't happening to me but rather it was just the way I thought. She seemed to be saying that I was responsible for my life and could have stopped some of the things from happening to me in the first place. And then to confirm it, she named this way of thinking. She called it a "victim mentality." I am sure if you could have seen the look on my face it would have been one of complete shock. I had never imagined such a thing. I had assumed everyone thought the way I did.

As I processed what the instructor was saying, I recognized for the first time that I had a victim mentality through which I viewed life. It was my filter for everything and it skewed my out-look, just like the way that wearing a pair of glasses with colored lenses would. She began her teaching by describing exactly how everything looked to me through those colored lenses. When I felt like she completely understood me, instead of sympathizing with me, she began to talk about the colored lenses. In essence, it was as if she reached across the table from me and removed a pair of colored glasses that I didn't know I was wearing. I saw my victim mentality for the first time.

If someone had tried to tell me that I had a thinking problem, I probably would have been highly offended, because it would have implied that I was somehow responsible for the situation I was in— in contradiction to everything I believed as a victim. *First of all, all of these bad things have happened to me, and now someone is blaming me for them?* I wouldn't have been able to accept it. The safety I felt in the atmosphere of the workshop and the trust I developed in the in-structor up to that point in the weekend enabled me to receive what she was teaching. It allowed a separation to happen between me and the way I thought. I could see what I had never seen before—that *I thought like a victim.*

A victim mentality is a belief system based on the lie that people are not responsible for their lives. Its premise is that they do not have control over what happens to them and therefore cannot be held accountable for the condition of their lives. In other words, *a victim believes that life just happens.* That belief forms the foundation for everything else they believe and they filter all information and experiences through it. They believe that they are subject to whatever life brings their way. People can be innocent victims of a circumstance or event such as a car accident or a robbery, where they truly do not have any control over what happened. These one-time incidents are not what I am referring to; I am talking about victimization as an ongoing way of life.

I realized that my life had been hijacked. I had been living under other people's control, other people's rule, and other people's power. I wasn't ruling over my life; I was serving a master. That much I knew. What I learned as I evaluated my life without my colored lenses on was news to me. I realized that I wasn't in the wrong place at the wrong time and I didn't have bad luck. I had a wrong way of thinking about myself and about my life. *Because of the way I thought, I had fully cooperated with the hijacking.* I had walked out of my marriage in response to the pain, but unless I completely changed the way I thought, I would find my way into more situations of abuse and dysfunction, whether in a relationship, a workplace, or my family. Even though I had recognized that pain is a signal and not an emotion, it wasn't enough. I had to change my way of thinking in order to break free.

I am so thankful for that experience because it began the destruction of the victim mentality that had set me up for captivity from an early age. It was one of the greatest turning points in my life. I was never the same from that moment forward, because it was at that moment that I recognized the existence of a victim mentality I didn't know was there—and when I did, I changed my mind. I had to reprocess everything I believed as I realized that life wasn't just happening to me and that I could actually participate in the process. *My vocabulary quickly expanded to include words like choices, consequences, desires, outcomes, control, and decisions.* The world looked entirely different.

A victim mentality is usually learned. It is a perspective, and as children we practice the perspective we are taught without ever being told it is a perspective. For this reason, most people with a victim mentality are unaware that they have it. They believe that everyone thinks the way they do. They don't know that there is another way to think. Even if they recognize that there could be another way, they don't feel that they have the power to change. Sometimes, at the extreme, people with a victim mentality like it that way. Often they see playing the victim role as a way of getting their needs met, so why would they give it up? They do not process that there could be a better way. They like the sympathy they get from it, and it feels easier not to take responsibility for their own lives.

Where did a victim mentality originate? It developed as a result of separation from God. Adam and Eve developed a victim mentality as a result of their independent actions or sin. If we look a little further into their response to God's questions in Genesis 3, we hear them express it. God asks, "Who told you that you were naked? Have you eaten from the tree whose fruit I commanded you not to eat?" Adam replies, "It was the woman You gave to me who gave me the fruit, and I ate it." So God turns to Eve and asks her, "What have you done?" And Eve replies "The serpent deceived me. That's why I ate it." Two people, made in the image of God, who they only knew to be good, make a bad choice. When God questions their actions, they pull out their blame gun and state very clearly, "We were victims. It wasn't our fault. We are not responsible." Today there are people everywhere living in this same mentality. They believe, just like Adam and Eve did, that they are victims and that their lives have just happened to them.

It is interesting that a victim mentality originated out of a bad relationship. What was Eve doing talking to a serpent? She had God to talk to and her husband to talk to. She chose to relate to a snake. She chose to entertain a snake's perspective on her life. One of the marks on victims' lives is that they typically go from one bad relationship or situation to another. They entertain people they weren't made to relate to. For every person in an abusive or dysfunctional relationship, there have been many people who have asked, "What does she see in him?" or "What is he doing hanging out with them?" It is clear to the outsider that they are involved with someone they shouldn't be. *If someone questions your relationships, instead of being defensive, it is wise to try to see things from another perspective.*

Logic tells us that one negative experience would be enough to keep someone from making the same kind of choices over again, but the opposite is true. Repeatedly, women flee abusive situations only to find their way into new relationships that are even worse. People declare bankruptcy and then apply for another credit card. Children of alcoholics grow up and leave home, vowing that their lives will be different from their parents'—yet they often marry into the same dysfunction they could not wait to get away from. From an outsider's perspective, it appears that there is an invisible force that attracts victims to the same kind of destruction over and over again. Is there an invisible magnet that repeatedly draws people to situations where they are enslaved or mastered by something? Do abuse victims have signs on their foreheads that say "Hurt Me"? No. But there is a victim mentality set up in the lives of people who have lived in dysfunctional relationships and suffered abuse. It has to be broken in order for them to experience real freedom.

＋）＝＋）＝＋）＝

One of the reasons victims appear to be magnets for abuse is that they are accustomed to how abusers think and act. They know all about unpredictable, irrational, tormenting behavior and they recognize it when they encounter it in someone new. While abuse is painful, it is also familiar, and anything familiar is comfortable. That comfort causes them to be attracted to the new relationship rather than repelled by it. When people have been intimate with something once, even if it is destructive or dysfunctional, they find it easy to be intimate with it again.

People can quickly find their way down paths they've traveled before. Over and over again, people fall into the arms of whatever is familiar to them including abuse, addiction, and trouble.

The second reason people continue to be mastered by cycles of abuse is that healthy relationships make them feel uncomfortable. It does not take much for us to feel uncomfortable. We put the same arm in first every time we put on a coat. It's not that it is difficult to put the other arm in first but we are not likely to do it, simply because it is uncomfortable. When victims meet people who do not behave in an abusive way toward them, they experience discomfort because they don't know what makes these people tick or what to expect from them. Typically, they reject healthy relationships before they even have an opportunity to get established, simply because they do not like to be uncomfortable. They go from one abusive partner to the next, one abusive friend to the next, one bad job to the next, or even one bottle of whiskey to the next—not because it is good, but because it is comfortable.

The third reason victims of abuse cannot develop healthy relationships is that they believe they have little or no value as a person. In the same way that people won't pay more for something than they think it is worth, people will not receive more than they think they are worth. When we hear the all too common responses of, "Oh, you shouldn't have" or "That's too much" when people are given a gift, what they are really saying is, "I'm not worth it." Abuse victims will disqualify themselves from relationships when they perceive they are being treated better than what they think they are worth. They cannot receive it.

It is important to understand that freedom doesn't come from starting over; freedom comes from changing your thinking. To successfully break free from whatever thinking pattern has mastered you, you must be willing to be uncomfortable until you get used to being treated properly. You have to face the discomfort and unfamiliarity of being treated with respect and value. You must stay the course long enough for new relationships to form. If you are unwilling to do this, eventually isolation will drive you back to what is familiar to you, no matter how destructive.

It is easy to recognize people with a victim mentality. Their life is a story of what's happened to them. Their conversations generally begin with the words, "Let me tell you what happened to me." Day after day, week after week, and month after month they relate the story of their lives; and although the characters may change, it is always told from the same perspective—what happened to them. It is as if they are describing a soap opera or a movie they have watched in that there is no mention of choices, consequences, or results. They are always the victim of the story.

This perspective reveals that people with a victim mentality don't feel responsible for any of the things that are happening; they believe they are subject to them. If questioned why they don't change things, they quickly defend themselves with one of a long list of excuses and go to great lengths to prove why they can't change anything about their circumstances. They are convinced they have no choice or power. The emotions most commonly expressed by people with a victim mentality are frustration, anger, and disappointment. These come out as they tell their story. They are usually offended by other people, feel as if they have been wronged, and someone owes them. They ask themselves, "Why me?"

Another sign of a victim mentality is the constant voice of complaint. An empowered person will act in the face of something that is not normal, but a person who has been hijacked will complain about it. Complaint is seldom a cry for help; more often it is just a way to relieve some of the pain without actually doing anything about it. I think this is the reason that God hates complaining so much—because it is the opposite of action. *"When the Lord heard your complaining, he became very angry..."* (Deuteronomy 1:34). We respond to people's complaint thinking it is a sign they want something to change, but they likely don't even realize they could do something about the problem.

I am very aware of any area of my life where I hear myself repeatedly complaining because it is a sign that something has hijacked me, and I need to deal with it. I can be free or I can be the victim. I can make things happen, or I can let them happen. The choice is mine. I would still find myself in abusive circumstances if I hadn't stopped thinking like a victim and letting life happen to me. My thinking enabled the abuse. I had to take charge of my life to make it stop. You too must take charge to stop being a victim.

Self-pity is a common indicator of a victim mentality. People caught in this thinking pattern feel sorry for themselves and are drawn to people who will be sympathetic toward them. It is important to recognize that while sympathy can be comforting, it doesn't change circumstances, and after someone has sympathized with them, they are still left with the same situation. Everyone's energy could have been better spent finding constructive solutions that would change things.

A victim mentality causes people to avoid those who confront them rather than sympathize with them. Just as Adam and Eve hid from God, a victim will hide from or avoid anyone who will ask them what they've done that has contributed to their circumstances or what they are going to do about the situation in which they are caught. When avoidance doesn't work, victims defend themselves by blaming someone else, just like Adam and Eve did. Even when they know they did something wrong, there will still be someone else to blame; if they had not done their part, the victim wouldn't have done their part, thereby making them not guilty. The serpent really did deceive Eve, but blaming him did not negate the consequences of Eve's choice. Adam blaming Eve did not negate the consequences of his choices. When confronted with what they had done, they had the opportunity to change the situation—but instead, they insisted on being victims of what happened and were stuck with the consequences. Anytime someone hides something, it is a sign that something is ruling over them, instead of them ruling over it. They are embarrassed that they have come under its control.

People who see themselves as victims are very selective in their focus. They have a negative perspective that sees the bad and not the good in life. They are seldom thankful because they cannot see what they should be thankful for. They see what everyone else has done wrong but not their own mistakes. They see the things they cannot control and ignore the things within their control. As a result of this limited focus, they stand vigilantly against change. They defend their perceived inability to make any changes with excuses for why things are the way they are. Solutions and advice are always meant for someone else. If they read a book, they apply it to someone else's life. If they go to church, they hear the sermon and think about who should have been there to hear it. They fail to see any application to their own lives because they have a victim mentality. They prefer making excuses to making decisions.

Life is very difficult when you have a victim mentality. It is exhausting and wearing because there is never any hope of change. It was such a relief to discover there is a better way of life. I was never the same after I attended that workshop and realized I had a victim mentality. As I embraced a new way of looking at things, it took time to process that into every area of my life, but there was a change in my identity that was irreversible.

I stopped being a victim when I didn't think so.

Chapter 12

BORN TO RULE

Victims aren't necessarily doing something wrong; they just have a case of mistaken identity. It's not enough to tell them not to think the way they do, because they are thinking exactly like victims do. It's their identity (who they are being) that is at the root of their behavior (what they are doing). They have to know who they really are in order to change and begin to think and act differently. They must see their true identity.

If you read the last chapter and realized that a set of colored glasses have been affecting your life like I did, then you may be wondering, *If I'm not a victim, then who am I? If life hasn't been just happening to me, then what has been going on?* You may feel relieved to have discovered that you've been living in the captivity of a victim mindset; but now that you have recognized that's not who you are, you need some answers.

The truth is you are not a victim; you are a ruler. You are the one in charge of your life. You are the one responsible for drawing the lines, making the rules, setting the boundaries, writing the script, playing the part, giving the commands and executing the plan—of *your* life. You always have been the one in charge; you just never got the memo. As a result, you've been living with a mistaken identity. You took on the identity, or role, of a victim, but it was a "mis-take." You were supposed to take the identity of a ruler. Every day when you should have been showing up to play the leading role in your story, you stayed in the audience and watched what happened.

I lived with a mistaken identity for the first twenty-seven years of my life. As a result of a victim mentality, I allowed life to rule me. It didn't get better as I got older; it got worse. I was smart and talented, but I had not been taught to rule. I had been taught how to be a victim. And I attracted into my life people who would victimize me. I read self-help books, I took self-esteem classes, but they all just told me to believe in myself—none of them actually had any power to change me because none of them addressed my identity. When I tried to apply what they said, I was a victim putting on someone else's outfit. I could only masquerade as a ruler.

You have to recognize that you actually are a ruler in order to think like one. It is an identity issue. If you think you are a victim, you will not rule no matter what your costume. When you understand that a ruler is who you are, then you will begin to think as a ruler thinks and act like a ruler acts. *Changing your behavior will not change your identity, but changing your identity will change your behavior.* When I understood that I was in charge of my life, when I understood I was a ruler and not a victim, I began to think differently and act differently—and success replaced failure.

How do we know that we are rulers? The Bible tells us we were made that way from the beginning. It's our God-given identity. We were all created to rule. We can prove it by going back to what things looked like in the world when humankind was created and before a victim mentality showed up.

According to Genesis 1, Adam was made in God's image and given dominion over the earth. To have dominion means to rule. That dominion had only one limitation. Genesis 2:16-17 says, *"But the Lord God warned him, 'You may freely eat the fruit of every tree in the garden—except the tree of the knowledge of good and evil. If you eat its fruit, you are sure to die.'"* He was telling Adam, "You weren't made for self-rule. You are in charge of the earth, but I'm in charge of you. If you decide to be independent, if you decide to rule on your own, your life will be destroyed." Adam immediately began to rule over the earth. The first thing he did was to name everything. We are told that God brought all the animals and birds to Adam to see what he would call them (see Genesis 2:19). If we think about that, a person has to be in charge of something to have the authority to name it. It is clear that Adam was ruling right from the start as he named all of the animals. He was created with the ability to determine the nature of things. God had authorized him to do so. As rulers over our own lives, we determine the nature of things. If we think we are victims, then that determines the nature of our lives.

Rulers have a very different mentality from victims. For them, life is internal rather than external. It is not something that is happening to them; they are making it happen. They know they are responsible for it. They see themselves as the authors of the stories, not storytellers. An author writes the story, but a storyteller can only retell what the author has already written. Rulers believe their lives are pictures of the choices and decisions they have made. They know they have power and control.

Rulers have a positive perspective. They recognize and focus on the good things in life and are able to express thankfulness for what they have. When things go wrong, they are able to evaluate why, and then take responsibility for the mistakes they have made. It is not a problem for them to take the blame for something. They focus on what they have control over and act accordingly. They see the choices they have available to them rather than the obstacles that oppose them. *They make decisions, not excuses.* When they want a different result, they make a different choice. They feel powerful in the context of ruling their own lives. People who rule are not exempt from trouble or pain, but they have little need for sympathy because they understand that sympathy doesn't bring change, only momentary comfort. They would never settle for comfort when they can do something about what is making them uncomfortable.

Rulers are able to forgive others when they fail or wrong them because they refuse to allow someone else to be in charge of their lives. Ruling makes it easy to let go of things and move forward. Rulers are open to and desire change, and they are creative in their approach to life. When they hear advice or a good sermon or read a good book, the first place they look to implement it is in their own lives. It excites them to make desired changes, and they feel good about it when they do. To sum it up, rulers have the mindset of a ruler; they rule over and are in charge of their lives.

Have you ever been asked to show identification to prove who you are? When the serpent approached Eve in the Garden and suggested that she eat from the forbidden tree, telling her it would make her like God, he was asking for her identification. He knew who she was, but he was asking if *she* knew who she was. He was asking, "Are you like God or aren't you?" and "Are you in charge or not?" He knew that as long as Eve believed she was like God, she was in charge of her world and he was powerless. But if the serpent could get her to believe she was something else, if he could get her to identify with something else, Eve would relinquish her authority and give up control of her life. That is exactly what happened. She became a victim when she took on the wrong identity.

Every time we are confronted with a situation or a problem or a decision, we get ID'd. We get asked for identification. The situation or problem or decision begs the question, "Who's in charge here?" We respond in one of two ways—either we are in charge or we are not in charge. We're rulers or we're victims. And whatever we identify with determines the outcome. *Either we take charge of the situation or the situation takes charge of us.* Whenever we respond with a victim ID, it's a case of mis-"taken" identity. We take on the identity of victims instead of rulers.

From this day forward, choose to believe that you are who God says you are. Refuse to believe anything to the contrary. Wash off all of the labels that other people have put on you. Don't answer to any other name except ruler. Don't let there be any more cases of mistaken identity in your life. The greatest challenge in doing this is usually your feelings because you can feel like an imposter when you begin to act like a ruler. The feelings will take care of themselves as you choose to live by truth rather than feelings. You are a ruler. You always have been; you just didn't know it. You're in charge—now rule your life!

In the Bible, a man named David modeled how to live a God-given identity in the face of opposition. (See First Samuel 16.) God had determined that David would be the next king. God sent a man named Samuel to find David and identify him publicly as the future king. God did not tell Samuel David's name; He only told him that he was one of the sons of Jesse. Samuel found Jesse and his sons, and prepared to carry out the ceremony, only to discover that David was not among the brothers; he was tending the sheep. David, God's chosen man, was excluded from the family gathering. No one who knew him saw any reason for him to be there, clearly indicating that no one recognized who David was in God's eyes. When David was summoned and told he would become king, he faced an identity crisis. He had to choose whether to align himself with his God-given identity as declared by Samuel or the mis-taken identity of insignificance endorsed by his father and his brothers. As far as we know, none of them even considered that it was possible for David to be the one for whom Samuel was looking. Their actions revealed their disbelief.

Have you ever faced this kind of rejection? Does your family see you as God does, or do they disqualify you? Do you wrestle with the mistaken identity that they have established? Are you the black sheep of the family or the one who can never get it right? Are you the insignificant one? Or are you the one criticized for daring to break the mold? These are all too common occurrences that often result in cases of mistaken identity. The opinions expressed by the people who are closest to us often speak the loudest, and many times we choose to identify with the way they see us instead of with the way God sees us.

David rose above his family's dismissal of him. He could have been discouraged, thinking that even his father didn't see anything in him. He could have disqualified himself based on the way his brothers regarded him. He could have wandered back to the sheep hanging his head and thinking he would never be anything more than a shepherd. Instead, David believed what God said about him and refused to allow his family's actions to define him. His battle was not with his family; his greatest challenge, as it is with any of us, was to rule over his own thoughts and emotions that opposed him. David embraced his God-given identity and acted accordingly. How did he do it? The Bible is full of accounts of the words David spoke to himself as he commanded his thoughts and emotions to submit to who he was.

> *Why am I discouraged? Why is my heart so sad? I will put my hope in God! I will praise him again—my Savior and my God!* (Psalm 42:11)

> *Be brave. Be strong. Don't give up. Expect God to get here soon* (Psalm 31:24 MSG).

> *I am not afraid of the thousands of enemies who surround me on every side* (Psalm 3:6 GNT).

> *When I lie down, I go to sleep in peace; you alone, O Lord, keep me perfectly safe* (Psalm 4:8 GNT).

> *Though a mighty army surrounds me, my heart will not be afraid...* (Psalm 27:3).

What we tell ourselves when people and circumstances oppose us is critical. Our identity is at stake. You begin to realize as you study how David lived that the biggest battles were not external; they were internal. No matter what opposed him, David had to win the battle with his emotions and his thoughts in order to keep ruling. We all have to do this.

Winning the battle within became a pattern for David, and it kept him on track through the challenges of life. He never forgot who he was even when he faced repeated attempts on his life, multiple counts of betrayal, and his own sins of adultery and murder. His identity, and not his circumstances or his feelings, determined his responses. This needs to be your pattern too.

After you have chosen to believe that you are who God says you are and to rule over your opposing thoughts and emotions, the next step is to understand and embrace the boundaries God has placed on your life. *You were meant to serve God and everything else was meant to serve you.* He created you to serve only one ruler—Him—and through that relationship, you receive the ability to rule your life. Time should serve you. Money should serve you. Things should serve you. Relationships should serve you. And these things will serve you, when you rule in life in relationship with God. Just like Adam and Eve, you were not created to live independently from God, but in close relationship with Him. When you submit your life to God's rule, you will be able to rule successfully over every aspect of your life.

As a ruler, you must take responsibility for your life. God gave one person dominion over your world—*you.* Accept that you are the one in charge of everything including your thoughts, your feelings, your home, your children, your marriage, your future, and your joy. It's up to you. Stop waiting for someone to give you permission to do the things you want to do or make the changes you want to make. You are in charge. Your past must be put in its place. Refuse to let it define you. The good times and the bad times alike are behind you, and you are powerless to do anything to change them. The way you rule over them is to move on. *Don't allow your past to steer your tomorrow.*

Stop playing the blame game. When you blame someone for something, you abdicate responsibility and mis-"takenly" assume the role of a victim. To be the ruler you were meant to be, you won't need or want to cast blame.

Leave your self-image behind. Adam and Eve had no self-image before they sinned. They saw themselves like God. They became self-conscious as a result of sin or being separated from God. Sin causes each person to develop a self-image and self-consciousness as well. You will bow down to whatever image you have developed in your mind because it is who you believe you are. If you refuse to see that self-image anymore and focus on who God says you are, you will act the way you are meant to act. You will rule.

You are responsible for your life. When you let go of your victim mentality and embrace responsibility, life won't just happen to you anymore; you will begin to make your life happen. You have choices and those choices have consequences. They may not always be easy or pleasant, but you do have choices. *Although you cannot control what happens to you, you can control how you respond.* Take ownership. No one, absolutely no one, can control your response except you. You have the power to not allow circumstances to rule you. Your thinking doesn't stop negative circumstances or events from happening, but it stops the circumstances from ruling you.

Any time you stop ruling over an area of your life, someone else will start. There is no place of neutrality. You can't just let things ride or see what happens. If you do, the other players will determine the course of events, taking you captive to their decisions. They are not the ones to blame for this. If you had been in charge, there wouldn't have been a place for them to occupy or take over. They wouldn't have been able to hijack *your* life.

⬥⬥⬥

My life changed so much in the first few years as I learned to take charge. I diligently adjusted the way I thought, always aligning it to what was true; and as a result, I was rebuilding my life. Then a season hit that I wasn't prepared for. I awoke early one Sunday morning to a phone call telling me that my grandfather had attempted suicide. I arrived at the hospital before the helicopter and was the first one allowed into the room upon his arrival. It was horrible to see my grandfather, bandaged and frantically struggling against the tubes in his throat and the restraints on his wrists. I couldn't tell if he was in pain from the gunshot wound to his chest or panic because he couldn't breathe or both. I could not calm him down and I felt overwhelmed and helpless. Reeling from shock, I stepped out of the room to try to get my bearings, but the next thing I knew I was looking up into the faces of the nursing staff. I had fainted. Over the next weeks, Grandpa lived in great torment and mental anguish. He never emotionally recovered and finally succumbed to death three months later.

That same month, I came home from a vacation with my son to the harsh news that he and his father were moving out of the area the next morning. Less than a month later, I collapsed on the floor at work in excruciating pain. I was taken to the hospital, but they sent me home, telling me nothing was wrong with me. Two days later, when the pain didn't stop, they did more tests that showed my organs were shutting down and my life was in jeopardy. I was wheeled to the operating room for emergency surgery. I began to regain my physical strength after a few weeks and eventually returned to work, but emotionally I didn't recover.

Burying my grandfather, saying a painful good-bye to my son, and having major surgery was simply too much for me to process. Unable to cope with the pain, I stopped feeling anything. For the next eight months, I was numb. I don't know how else to describe it except to say that I felt absolutely nothing. In this constant state of suppressed pain, each day was a choice whether or not to revert to my "default setting" and begin playing the victim once more. I could easily have gone down the hopeless, helpless path of wondering *Why me?* and *How could these things have happened?*, but I refused to succumb. I made the conscious choice to keep going to church and to keep reading my Bible. I knew there was life in those choices even though I felt absolutely nothing from either one of them. Week after week, month after month, I just went through the motions of life, continuing to feel nothing. I didn't know how to get back to normal; all I knew to do was to keep committed to the way of life I had chosen before these tragedies happened.

Eventually, I reached out for some help. The dark days came to an end when a friend prayed for me. I began to feel again. I know without a doubt that if I had succumbed to my feelings during that time, if I had stopped going to church or reading God's Word, I would have lost the battle. I would have eventually turned to something else for comfort and set myself up once again to be taken hostage by another hijacker.

No matter what you are going through, please do not give up. Refuse to let your feelings rule you. Consciously make good choices, and reach out for help. You will come through if you persevere and choose life. You have to learn how to rule the way you were intended. It is time to stop letting life happen to you and start making life happen. You are not a victim; you are a ruler. You can begin ruling today. Just like the director of a movie does when things aren't going right, you can yell, "Cut!" and start the scene over again. This time you will write the story. This time there won't be any mis-"taken" identity. This time you will play the lead.

One of the things that I love about Christianity is that it has taught me who I am in Christ and how to rule over my life. Ephesians 2:6 says, *"In our union with Christ Jesus he raised us up with him to rule with him in the heavenly world"* (GNT). As a result, I am passionate about teaching people to rule so that they can really live the way Jesus intended them to as He said in John 10:10, *"...I have come that they may have life, and that they may have it more abundantly"* (NKJV). I hate it when I see life ruling people. I hate it when I see people who are oppressed with anything from not being able to pay their bills to not being able to get out of bed because they are depressed. Should addiction rule them? Should fear rule them? Should rejection? *I don't think so.* I won't accept people's excuses about why they can't overcome because I know they were born to rule. If I could change and if I can rule, they can too. They just need the right identification.

Chapter 13

WHAT GIVES YOU THE RIGHT?

Have you ever experienced anxiety when a police officer, a customs official, or even a restaurant server asks for your identification? It can be unnerving. It is not that you are unsure of your identity. It is that you wonder if you really have the right to do what you are trying to do. That question can cause you to lose your confidence.

One of my friends returned to Canada from an international trip, happy to have landed at the airport and looking forward to arriving home. However, when he presented his identification to the customs official, he was promptly escorted to another room and arrested because of an outstanding warrant that he knew nothing about. There were charges against him that interfered with his right to get back into the country. Even though the situation was a result of someone's mistake and everything was eventually sorted out, my friend still experiences stress every time he travels and has to clear customs. He wonders if some accusation or charge will have been made against him. He knows his identification is correct, but he is plagued by the fear that maybe he won't have the right to enter.

The same thing can happen to you when you begin to live in your true identity as a ruler. Circumstances can arise that cause you to wonder if you really have the right to rule over things. Charges and accusations can come your way that cause you to lose your confidence, just like my friend did.

We naturally operate this way, especially when we are used to thinking like victims. We discover Jesus died to forgive our sins and restored us to a place of dominion, and we rejoice. But then, if we begin to think about ourselves, our failures, shortcomings and sins, our past behavior or our weaknesses, we can quickly misplace what was given to us and come up with a list of things that disqualify us from ruling. A battle ensues between understanding that we are rulers and knowing that we have inadequacies. As we entertain the charges against us, guilt and condemnation become our accusers. They rob us of confidence and we wonder how we can stand up to our hijackers and say that we are in control now. Whenever charges cause us to be unsure of our rights, we will lack confidence in ruling effectively.

Often what happens under that pressure is that we move into justification. We acknowledge our failures by justifying ourselves. To justify means to prove to be right, just or reasonable, to pronounce free from guilt or blame. Every time we begin a statement with the words, "I just," we aren't denying the charges against us, but we are making an excuse that we believe cancels out their effect, instead of just being honest about our failure. The truth is that justifying something does not negate its effects. If you can justify why you were late, you were still late. If you can justify why you overspent, you still overspent. If you can justify why you didn't exercise, you still didn't exercise. If you can justify why you didn't do what your boss asked you to do, you still didn't do what your boss asked you to do. And you still have the consequences. All you did was allow your failure to hijack you because you can't change what you excuse or justify.

Some people think life is a series of justifications. They miss it, time after time, with justification after justification. You were not made for excuses. *You are to rule, and God is to justify.* He wants to free you from the hijacker known as justification. Freedom comes from understanding God has already chosen to justify you, so you do not have to justify your behavior. This truth is found in Romans 8:33, *"Who dares accuse us whom God has chosen for his own? No one— for God himself has given us right standing with himself."* Do not live under the captivity of justification. Refuse to justify yourself. Give that responsibility back to God.

If you aren't going to justify yourself, then what do you do with the guilt and condemnation that come from failures and sins? If we stop justifying, doesn't that take us back to a place of losing our confidence in our right to rule? Yes, it does. In order to overcome this, and truly defeat a victim mentality, you have to understand what gives you the right to rule so that you never waiver. Certainly you have rights according to the laws of the land, but the right to exercise dominion over your life, rather than being a victim, comes from God Himself. Your right to rule comes from being "righteous" or in right standing with God.

Adam and Eve gave our dominion, our right to rule, away when they sinned. God had given them authority over everything in the world, but they gave away their authority to the serpent. The whole purpose of Jesus and His death on the cross was to restore to humankind the dominion that comes through a right relationship with God. The cross wasn't just about saving us from hell; it was about restoring us to our proper place, a place of dominion. Jesus made an exchange when He chose to die on the cross. He exchanged His righteousness for our sin. He took our place and gave us His. He became sin and we became righteous in one transaction. Jesus gave us His identity, His credentials: *"For God made Christ, who never sinned, to be the offering for our sin, so that we could be made right with God through Christ"* (2 Corinthians 5:21). We no longer live under our own identity of a sinful nature. We received His nature; and it is in His identity that we receive the right to rule. We stand in His righteousness against which no accusation can be made. No matter who questions our authority, His righteousness is sufficient to put all charges against us to rest. Man gave his dominion away and God paid to get it back. Through Jesus, our righteousness and our rights were restored.

When we believe that Jesus took our place on the cross, forgave our sin, and gave us His righteousness, we overcome sin. Romans 5:17 says, *"If death got the upper hand through one man's wrongdoing, can you imagine the breathtaking recovery life makes, sovereign life, in those who grasp with both hands this wildly extravagant life-gift, this grand setting-everything-right, that the one man Jesus Christ provides?"* (MSG).

I didn't understand this whole truth initially. I grasped quite readily that Jesus died in my place, took the punishment for my sins, and forgave my sins when I received Him as my Savior. It was amazing to know that I was cleansed of every sin I had ever committed, every mistake I had ever made, and every failure I had ever experienced. It did not mean that all of the consequences of those things were removed; but I knew Jesus had taken the punishment for my sin and I was forgiven. He had wiped the slate clean of all the charges of sin that were against me: *"the slate wiped clean, that old arrest warrant canceled and nailed to Christ's Cross"* (Colossians 2:14 MSG).

If a friend offered to take my place and relieve me of some responsibility such as doing my job, I would be released from my obligation, but my identity wouldn't change. This was how I saw what Jesus had done for me. It was an incomplete picture. What Jesus did in taking my place was just one side of the transaction. The other side was that when Jesus became sin, I became righteous. He took my identity and gave me His. Romans 8:1 says, *"So now there is no condemnation for those who belong to Christ Jesus."* I didn't understand that. I didn't know He had given me His credentials, and so I did not live this way. I lived as though I had been forgiven, but I kept what I thought was my sinful identity. I believed that it was up to me to perform well at all times in order to remain in right standing with God. When I would do something I knew I shouldn't, it was difficult to move past it. First John 1:9 says, *"If we confess our sins, He is faithful and just to forgive us our sins and to cleanse us from all unrighteousness"* (NKJV). I would confess it, but I also thought I had to do a whole lot of good things in order to get back into right standing with God again. I would find it difficult to pray if I had sinned and would wrestle with my guilty conscience.

When you lose something precious that you have no ability to get back, it is an incredible relief when someone returns it to you. There is heartfelt thankfulness and joy that things have been put back in their rightful place. However, if you misplace that thing again, you will revert back to the fear and anxiety of having lost it. That's what I was doing. When I received Jesus' forgiveness, I was so relieved and thankful for His costly gift. But I did not know how to move forward in that. As long as I was doing well, I had confidence to rule, but any time I failed or sinned, I lost confidence. The more I stumbled, the harder I worked to compensate. The pressure of having to perform became greater and greater. I was still living under the power of a lie—that I could work out my righteousness.

Adam and Eve were made righteous, or in the image of God. It was not a result of anything they did. When the serpent suggested to Eve that she would be like God if she did something (take from the forbidden tree), Eve responded like most of us do. She forgot that righteous was something she was, and made it something she did. She tried to *do* something to make herself be like God: righteous. I had done the very same thing. I had been deceived into thinking that being righteous was something I could do, instead of believing it was something I was given. Second Corinthians 5:21 says, *"God made him who had no sin to be sin for us, so that in him we might become the righteousness of God"* (NIV). I had been trying to earn something I already was.

When Jesus died, He was redeeming humankind's righteousness and authority the same way it had been lost, through an exchange. Jesus became sin but it wasn't by sinning. He never sinned to become a sinner. He exchanged the state He was in for the state humankind was in. Once that exchange was made, when people receive Christ's gift of salvation, they exchange their sin for His righteousness. So the moment I received Christ, I became righteous. I got my rights back. I received them in exchange for my sin. My righteousness was a gift from Jesus. In relationship with Jesus, God sees me as righteous.

Romans 6:18 says, *"You were set free from sin and became the slaves of righteousness"* (GNT). Righteousness is not something you can do or earn! You become righteous through receiving salvation. You can't add anything to it. It cannot be attained any other way. You can never be any more righteous than you were the moment you received Christ. Romans 10:3 says, *"For they don't understand God's way of making people right with himself. Refusing to accept God's way, they cling to their own way of getting right with God by trying to keep the law."*

We are born with a sinful nature. We did not do anything to become sinners. Of course, we all eventually commit sins in our lives, but that is not what makes us sinners. In the same way, once I receive Christ and His righteousness, there is nothing I can do to add or take away from my righteousness because Jesus is my righteousness. That truth brought great freedom to me and lifted the burden of guilt that had been growing in my life as I worked to be righteous in God's sight. I did not have to perform anymore. I desire to live as righteously as I can, but that is not what gives me right standing with God. Jesus gave me right standing with God. First Corinthians 15:34 says, *"Awake to righteousness, and do not sin; for some do not have the knowledge of God..."* (NKJV).

Anytime I find myself trying to perform for God, with my motive being to make myself right before Him, I am reminded of Galatians 2:21: *"...For if keeping the law could make us right with God, then there was no need for Christ to die."*

You cannot rule without righteousness. When you don't know who gives you your rights, as soon as an accusation is made, you will lose your confidence, making it impossible to stand your ground. The Bible describes righteousness as a piece of armor called a breastplate. It covers your chest, protecting your heart and your emotions and enables you to stand strong. Ephesians 6:14 says, *"Stand your ground, putting on the belt of truth and the body armor of God's righteousness."* Righteousness shields your heart from the torment of guilt and condemnation.

It is truly freeing to know that the right to rule over your life comes from what Jesus did and nothing else. Let this truth sink deep into your heart. You must know it so you are not taken captive again by your own thinking. Stop trying to be something you already are. *Know your rights and be the ruler you were meant to be.*

Chapter 14

OVERCOMING REJECTION

I was born rejected. How could that be? No one even knew me yet. I was unplanned, unexpected. As a result, there was quite a reaction when my existence became known. Words of rejection were spoken over my life by some; words that said I should be abandoned or my life should be terminated. Not all of the words spoken sounded like this but those words were enough for me to be born with a sense of rejection.

It really wasn't about me. I hadn't done anything. I didn't have any choice in my existence. There was nothing wrong with me. It was about shame and guilt and what people would think. It was about anger and fear and disappointment. It had nothing to do with me and everything to do with the other people involved. Nevertheless, even though I did not know the facts, I had a sense of being rejected; I had a sense that I was undesirable and unacceptable, right from the beginning. I received rejection into my identity.

What is rejection? It can be a real event where a person is rejected in some way, but more often rejection is a way of thinking or a perception of self. It is very much feelings-based. We perceive it and so we feel it. We can produce the emotion of rejection even if it did not really happen. Rejection is inward and self-focused; it evaluates everything in relationship to one's self. Rejection in a person's life makes everything all about them, and it is based on a lack of self-worth. Ironically, rejection continually seeks acceptance, yet expects to find rejection in the process. In looking outward for approval, we are really seeking to confirm that we don't measure up. We gauge our interaction with people based on whether or not they are rejecting us.

Rejection twists everything as it tries to validate itself. It is only satisfied when it finds proof of its existence. It robs people of their sense of worth and belonging. It starts with an incident but it becomes a way of life, putting a person on an insatiable search for proof of the rejection that they believe marks them. Once people believe they are rejected, they lose their ability to tell the difference between real and perceived rejection.

According to the dictionary, *reject* means "to refuse to accept (someone or something); to rebuff, to discard as useless or unsatisfactory…".[1] That was what I experienced. I was refused, rebuffed, discarded as useless or unsatisfactory by the opinions of others before I was even born. Rejection is a common result of illegitimacy; the baby has no legal right to be. Other factors at birth can produce rejection. Perhaps you were unplanned or unwanted. You may have been given up for adoption or your mother may have attempted an abortion. Your parents may have wanted a child of the opposite sex. Or your parents may have been upset at your existence because they were not in a position financially or emotionally to be caring for a baby or another baby. Perhaps your father abandoned you or never even knew you existed. Perhaps you were born with a health issue that your parents were not prepared for. Even when a child is loved, sensing that the parents are somehow disappointed can be enough to produce rejection in that child.

Rejection can result from the atmosphere of the home you were born into. Home environments can be unstable or abusive for a variety of reasons. Parents might not have the skills to raise a child. They may withhold love. Their expectations might be too high or they might compare the child unfairly to another sibling. The parents might quarrel a lot or be physically or emotionally abusive. Mental illness, extended sickness, and the death of a parent are traumatic. So is divorce. Traumatic events can transmit a message of rejection to a child.

Rejection can exist in a family for generations. Children learn to think and speak the lifestyle of rejection modeled to them as they grow up.

Very few people reach adulthood without receiving some mark of rejection. Growing up, your physical appearance might have been rejected. Maybe you reached puberty much earlier or much later than your peers. Maybe you were poor. Maybe you were rich. Maybe you were too fat, or maybe you were too skinny. You might have been rejected by a boyfriend or girlfriend and your femininity or masculinity was rejected. If you've been divorced, fired, or hurt by a friend, you have been rejected. Perhaps you failed at something or made a mistake that caused people to reject you. Rejection always produces a sense of feeling as though you are unacceptable. We are not usually rejected for something we have done; it is generally something about our nature that gets rejected. That gives rejection power because we can change our actions, but we cannot change who we are. *When we identify with rejection, we are helpless to do anything about it, and we become its victim.*

Everyone gets rejected one way or another. When rejection happens, we have a choice whether or not to receive it. Some people process rejection as part of life and choose to be unaffected. They recognize that they were rejected, but they do not allow it to affect how they see themselves. However, when we experience rejection and we allow what happened to be a reflection of ourselves, we receive rejection into our very identity and it becomes a way of life. From that point on, we are unable to think about ourselves without seeing rejection. It is one thing to experience rejection; it is another thing to become rejected and identify yourself that way. Experiencing rejection doesn't take us into captivity, but identifying with rejection does.

If you have been taken captive by rejection, there probably was something really valid that happened, some intense point of rejection where that belief about yourself was given access. Rejection happens. The danger is in how we respond. As long as rejection is just something someone did to us, it does not take control over us. But *the moment we believe we are rejected, it changes from an experience to an identity*. At that point it hijacks our lives because it has become part of who we are. From that point on, we sense rejection in every relationship because it is how we see ourselves. When a busy person doesn't have time to talk to us, when someone doesn't notice us, or when someone doesn't include us, we believe it is because something is wrong with us. It is all about us.

When we are hijacked by rejection, we have allowed an experience to rob us of our sense of worth and belonging. We don't even need another instance of rejection to remain hijacked because we are already rejecting ourselves on an ongoing basis. *Perceived rejection is far more damaging than real rejection, because it is all in our minds.* In that hidden place, it will never be confronted and never be resolved. We perceive it and suffer the pain of it sometimes without anyone else even knowing. We are rejecting ourselves so it really does not matter too much how other people treat us; we experience the pain of rejection continually.

The symptoms of rejection mostly manifest in relationships. Rather than living in genuine, authentic relationships, victims of rejection believe everything that happens in the relationship is about them. They assume other people's motives, and they are sure they know what the other person is thinking toward them. They know why some person didn't talk to them, why the waiter didn't smile at them, why another driver looked at them a certain way in traffic, why someone didn't return their call, and so on. It is always because of some deficiency they see in themselves. They are thinking for both parties, and an imaginary relationship exists in their minds that the other people know nothing about. They invest a lot of energy calculating what is going on in the thoughts and intentions of the other person. Every look, gesture, and tone of voice is intensely scrutinized in a search to find the rejection they are sure is there. They seldom ask what the other person is really thinking, and if they do, they don't believe they are being honest anyway. Their own belief about themselves will override what the other person says.

I have had a close friend who, for personal reasons, did not invite me to the ceremony when she got married. As a teenager, my friend had a baby out of wedlock and experienced much judgment and shame for being an unwed mother. Her husband-to-be loved her little girl and was going to adopt her at the wedding ceremony. Because it was very private to them, they chose not to have other people at the ceremony, including me. Since I lived under the control of rejection, I misunderstood her actions. Like any other person hijacked by rejection, I assumed that it was all about me. When she did not invite me to the ceremony, I took on even more rejection, and so I decided to deal with it by not going to the reception either. When she found out I wasn't coming, she called to express her disappointment. I did not soften my stance at all; I was sure she had rejected me, and so I refused to go. I withdrew from the relationship, and it was the end of my friendship with her—all because I believed everything was about me. It wasn't about me at all, but I got exactly what I believed.

People who believe they are rejected are unable to receive love, even though that is what they desperately want. They are convinced they are unlovable, so when someone demonstrates love toward them, it is almost impossible for them to receive it. They do not believe it is genuine and they reject it. Or they believe it is just a matter of time until the other person realizes they are unworthy of love or affection. As a result, they respond to love, affection, and generosity by trying to repay it. If someone does something for them, they try to make it up to them because they cannot simply receive it. They continually keep score to ensure that they never receive more than they have given. They can't receive more because if they did, it would violate their belief that they are rejected.

One summer I was trying to get ready to go on a long trip. I had a toddler who was very demanding, and I was overwhelmed by everything that needed to be done by the next morning. One of my friends offered to come over and help; but when she came, I could not let her do anything because I felt I was undeserving of her help. When she insisted, I finally conceded that she could do the dishes. It was just too much for me to receive anything more. After all, I was rejected. How could I act like I wasn't?

Broken relationships commonly mark the lives of rejected people. As soon as there is conflict or perceived rejection, they act out their rejection by withdrawing from the relationship.

Disagreement equates to rejection, rather than a realization that they might just have a difference of opinion. Any confrontation is perceived as a personal attack rather than a healthy process of life that enables people to deal with issues and move on. Another reason for broken relationships is that they reject people before the people can reject them. They are sure it is coming, so they decide to get it over with by initiating it themselves. New relationships seem fine in the beginning. But once they develop to a certain level, they become uncomfortable because they have started to care about the other person and know they are vulnerable to this person rejecting them. Rather than risking it, they may quietly withdraw from the relationship or even pick a fight to bring the relationship to a conclusion.

In his early teens, my son experienced some severe rejection that caused him to believe he would be rejected by everyone. I did not know anything had happened, but I knew that for a whole school year he spent almost all of his time alone. It was painful to watch and not be able to do anything to help. The following year he changed schools, and there were some guys in his new school that he already knew. For the first few weeks of school, he was with them a lot. He was bringing them home at lunch time and after school; but after about three weeks, I could sense him withdrawing. It was not because of any conflict or because he wasn't enjoying their company. Eventually he confided in me that when he had started junior high at a previous school, he had been severely bullied and mocked and told that no one wanted him there. It deeply wounded him, and from that point on he believed he was not wanted among his peers. Even though that bully was no longer in his life, the rejection identity kept him trapped in the pain of that experience, and he was now rejecting these new relationships before they could reject him. He was producing what he believed.

Rejected people treat others as though they too feel rejected. They give others what they themselves want. They can be overly caring or even smothering, thinking they are doing a good thing. When their behavior is rejected because it is overwhelming, they cannot handle it and the cycle of rejection repeats itself. Again, they aren't functioning in a real relationship, because they are thinking and feeling for both parties.

Rejection causes people to avoid circumstances or settings where they think they may be rejected. People find their identities in things such as work or money. If they find themselves in a position where they cannot hide behind any of these things, they will exit. For people who get their identity from their work, they can be confident as long as they are in an environment where their position is recognized. But if they find themselves in a completely social setting, disengaged from their work, rejection will rear its ugly head and cause them to feel unacceptable.

Rejected people are highly introspective. They are always looking at themselves and focusing on the things about themselves that they perceive to be undesirable. They see flaws that are invisible to anyone else. It could be the size of their nose or the color of their hair. It could be the sound of their voice or the way that they run. It may have come from being teased; they may have simply noticed they were different from someone else. They determined that they don't like their personality, their voice, their life, their family, etc. They aren't as slim, athletic, or talented as they think they should be. Every other person becomes a point of comparison against which they measure themselves to see if they are better or worse than that person in that area.

Another way rejection manifests is in perfectionism. *People falsely believe that if they are perfect, they cannot be rejected.* They have to do everything just right because all of their value is based on never making a mistake. It is a fallacy, because we can never control other people's perception of us or response to us. To think that we can behave well enough to stop rejection is deception. Rejection also manifests in performance. People spend their lives working or performing in order to make up for their perceived inadequacies. They try to earn what they should receive through relationship.

It is just as difficult to have a relationship with God as it is with others when you believe you are rejected. How can you come into God's presence and expect to be loved by Him when you know you are rejected? Rejected people usually find it very difficult to pray in the light of this expectation. That's not how it's supposed to be.

⊰—⊱—⊰

So what do you do if you have been hijacked by rejection? First of all, you must let go of the pain of any real rejection that has happened in your life. I experienced some deep pain when a boyfriend abruptly ended our relationship. He was a great person, and I really thought he liked me. I felt comfortable to be myself around him, and I opened my heart to him. When he rejected me, the pain was horrible. No matter how I rationalized everything or how hard I tried to move on, the tears would not seem to stop, and I was struck by panic attacks that would paralyze me. This went on for a few months, and no matter how hard I tried to move past the rejection, nothing I did made any difference. Then one day I read this verse in the Bible about Jesus: *"He is despised and rejected by men, a Man of sorrows and acquainted with grief..."* (Isa. 53:3a NKJV). Jesus was rejected by men. It says it again in First Peter 2:4, *"...rejected by humans but chosen by God and precious to him"* (NIV). Jesus knew the pain I was feeling. He endured the sorrow and grief that results from rejection. I had never heard that or understood it before. That truth was an antidote for the pain I was in. I felt my heart release the pain of that experience. I knew I didn't have to carry it anymore because He had carried it for me, and I was freed from that sorrow. Whatever the pain is that you are experiencing from rejection in your life, Jesus has known that pain, too, in order that you might be released from it. Allow Him to carry it for you. Know that you may have been rejected by people—but you are always precious to God.

Second, you must accept God's love for you. You are God's idea, God's design, and God's creation. How can you be more accepted than that? Ephesians 1:4-6 says, *"...Long before he laid down earth's foundations, he had us in mind, had settled on us as the focus of his love, to be made whole and holy by his love. Long, long ago he decided to adopt us into his family through Jesus Christ. (What pleasure he took in planning this!) He wanted us to enter into the celebration of his lavish gift-giving by the hand of his beloved Son"* (MSG). When we recognize God's love for us, it no longer matters who loves us or who doesn't. It won't matter if someone does reject us. God is the One who breathed life into each of us. Two people can have sex; that doesn't produce life. God's presence is what produces life. It doesn't matter who wanted you or planned you or didn't want you or didn't plan you; God is the One who decided you would be. Psalm 139:16 says, *"You* [God] *saw me before I was born. Every day of my life was recorded in your book. Every moment was laid out before a single day had passed."*

Decide to stop comparing. Comparison was never meant to be a game to play. We are constantly bombarded with images and messages that tempt us to compare our looks, our popularity, our stature, our income, our ability, our possessions, our personality, and our relationships to those of others. Comparison is destructive, because the result of comparison is that you are either better than someone else, or worse than someone else. Being better than someone else produces only temporary confidence, because at any moment there will be someone else to compare yourself to.

And of course, when you compare yourself and find that you don't measure up, you feel defeated. You can never win playing the game of comparison. *Accept your uniqueness.* I grew up thinking that if someone was different from me, then something was wrong with one of us. That made life extremely stressful, because either something was wrong with me or something was wrong with the other person. Now I understand that we are all uniquely made and not meant to be compared with one another. If people have something in their lives that we admire or desire, then they should be models to us of how to achieve that particular thing. They should not be a measure of our failure. Overcoming rejection means asking questions about how they accomplished something or how they obtained what they have.

In order to fully overcome rejection, you must stop seeking approval. One day, while shopping for a birthday card for a friend, the words on a particular card captured my attention. The verse began, "If you can value truth over approval...." As I tried to process what it said, there was a head-on collision with this thought and what I personally believed. I reread it several times. Value truth over approval? Why would I want to do that? Isn't approval the most important thing there is? Doesn't everyone want approval? Why would someone want truth instead? I placed high value on approval. It was very important to me to please others and ensure they were happy with me. As long as people thought well of me, I felt good about myself. But whenever something went wrong and I displeased someone, whether intentionally or accidentally, I saw it as a sign of failure. Anxiety and turmoil would grip me, and I would find it difficult to focus on anything else until I felt I had regained that person's approval. I paid more attention to what others thought of me than what I felt or desired. I was always on the lookout for any sign of someone's displeasure. If a person withdrew from me, or acted differently toward me than they usually did, I jumped to the conclusion that they were unhappy with me, and I began to analyze everything I could have possibly said or done to offend them. If I couldn't come up with anything, then I would do something like compliment them or try to make them laugh to see if I could get a positive reaction. I couldn't stand not knowing whether or not they were upset with me.

Since approval was so important, not only did I constantly seek it, I always worked hard to give it. I never wanted anyone else to feel like I disapproved of them. I would never tell someone the truth at the expense of hurting their feelings. If someone got a new haircut and I didn't like it, I said I did anyway because I wouldn't want to make them feel badly. If someone invited me to do something, I made up an excuse instead of saying I didn't want to because I didn't want them to be hurt. I conformed my opinions and actions into the framework of other people's feelings. In other words, I was dishonest.

In living for approval, I never felt safe. Since I was not honest, I did not think anyone else was either. No matter how positive someone acted toward me, I was always suspicious that they didn't really mean it. I could never let my guard down because no matter how many times I earned someone's approval, the next time could be the time that I would fail. Approval could be snatched away in an instant. Reading the birthday card that day caused me to realize that valuing approval was a mindset rather than a normal way of thinking. Believing I needed approval was a lie that affected all of my relationships. At first it was shocking to imagine that I did not have to live my life seeking approval, and that I wasn't bound to give it. What? Tell the truth and risk not being liked by everyone? Tell the truth and risk hurting someone's feelings? Let someone reject me? The thought was horrifying to me because I lived for approval and perceived even constructive truth as rejection.

I began to ask myself more questions. What if I could be okay whether people approved of me or not? What if I didn't have to live in anxiety if someone was unhappy with me? What would happen if I actually expected truth from people? What if I was truthful with people? What kind of result would that produce?

If people were honest with me, they might address something that was wrong with me or some flaw in my character. They might tell me they did not like my hair or did not approve of a choice I made. While that had some risk of pain attached to it, it was offset by the realization that at least then I would have the opportunity to do something about my problem rather than just pretending to be perfect. Instead of having to find a way to earn their approval, I could just evaluate their opinion, and if I agreed with it, I could fix the problem. If I didn't agree, I could be confident in who I was, without their approval.

I began to understand how valuable truth is. *Seeking truth rather than approval meant that I would not always have to be on guard, wondering what people were really thinking.* I could trust that if something was wrong, they would let me know; and I could trust that they really meant what they were saying. As I embraced a new perspective of valuing truth over approval, I no longer had to worry if I had broccoli in my teeth or my skirt tucked in my underwear because someone would tell me. I no longer spent time wondering if I had offended someone if they didn't stop and talk to me in the grocery store or if they didn't call. I now believed that they would tell me if there was a problem, and I didn't have to go imagining one. I was free to be honest with them as well. I enjoyed the newfound freedom of saying, "I don't feel like going out tonight, but thanks for thinking of me." Being real with people felt so liberating!

Allowing people to be honest with me regarding the strengths and the weaknesses they saw in me enabled me to discover that I still had value even where I was flawed. The pressure to be perfect lifted, and I began to feel safe in relationships for the first time. Truth became precious, because good or bad, truth can be processed. Truth means I can see things as they really are and make choices accordingly. Truth is far more valuable than approval ever will be. I've stopped wondering if people are mad at me, because I don't think so! *"And you shall know the truth, and the truth shall make you free"* (John 8:32 NKJV).

You must stop identifying with rejection. Stop believing you are rejected. Recognize that it is not always about you. In fact, it is hardly ever about you. People live life and make choices primarily based on themselves, not someone else. The majority of things that happen are simply not about us. They are not personal. They affect us, but they are just not about us. *Your identity must come from God, not from other people or other people's treatment of you.* The way other people treat you is usually about them. They are primarily motivated by what is good for them, not by what they think of you. You must stop thinking for them (making their actions about you) and let them make the choices they want to make. That's how you stop identifying with rejection. When a friend is busy and you don't hear from him or her, grasp that it is about the fact that he or she is busy—it is not about you. *It's not about me* should become your new life sentence. Every time you are tempted to reject yourself based on someone else's behavior, stop and tell yourself, *It's not about me.*

Rejection stops when you don't think so.

ENDNOTE

1. Dictionary.com, Dictionary.com Unabridged, Random House, Inc., s.v., "reject,"
http://dictionary.reference.com/browse/reject (accessed February 11, 2013).

Chapter 15

FACE YOUR ENEMY

Whe n a hijacking takes place, no one ever says, "Maybe the
hijacker will just go away." Or "Let's just wait and see
what happens." They know someone has to face the
enemy, and the sooner the better for the sake of the hostages! *Freedom only comes through confrontation.* But many people who find
themselves in the midst of trouble or circumstances do just the opposite—they avoid the enemy, hoping it will just go away.

Discovering that I needed to face my enemies was one of the
biggest lessons I had to learn in life. I was good at passing tests, but
I had never learned to prepare for a battle. I did not even know I was
supposed to battle. I did my best to avoid conflict, because I did not
know there was another option. Usually, I just waited for trouble to
go away. When you don't think you are the one in charge, you don't
stand up to face the problems. I never realized that I was responsible
to deal with my problems.

This is not uncommon. We live in a 9-1-1 world. At the first sign
of trouble, we call for help. Our homes and workplaces are wired
with all kinds of monitors and security systems with buttons to be
pushed and alarms to be sounded in the face of a threat. The police,
the fire department, and the paramedics are only minutes away in
any sort of danger or crisis. Their existence reinforces our false beliefs that someone else will solve our problems for us. We have great
confidence in their ability to rescue us. Nine-one-one is useful if

your house is on fire, if you have a medical emergency, or if a crime is being committed; but it does not work when we encounter the enemies of abuse, fear, sickness, rejection, addiction, and lack. Since there is no security system that can deliver us from these problems, we spend a lot of time complaining about these hijackers with the expectation that if we complain enough, maybe someone will come and do something about them. While we wait for the hijackers to go away or for someone to rescue us, the hijackers capture us because we fail to realize that we are the ones with the power to overcome. Stop looking around the room for someone else to be your savior, and recognize that *you alone have the power to defeat your enemies.*

If I were alone in a room with a bully and someone came along and dealt with the bully, it would be a good thing, but it would not solve my problem. It would be a temporary fix to something that needed a permanent solution. The best thing someone could do for me would be to come into the room and teach me how to face that bully and defeat him myself. Initially, it might seem cruel and hardhearted to take such a stance, but the most life-giving thing someone could do would be to teach me to overcome my enemy myself. The victory would become mine; and if the bully ever returned, I would know what to do. But if people just take care of the bully for me, they cripple me by making me dependent on them to solve my problems.

If God removed your enemy right now, would you be free? What if He removed your ex-boyfriend, your abusive parent, your difficult boss, or the teacher who ridiculed you? You would not be free at all. There would just be a temporary season of peace until another enemy made its way into your life. True freedom comes from knowing we can face any enemy that opposes us and come out victorious.

If you are learning this truth for the first time, your initial response might be panic because it is so foreign to how you have lived your life. Just the thought of facing your enemy can make you nauseous. Do not be alarmed; you do not have to do it alone. There are people who can teach you what to do and walk through the process with you; but you must understand that victory comes only when we confront. We are intended to arm ourselves with the necessary weapons, look our enemies straight in the eye, and defeat them. *When you face your enemy, God can empower you to defeat it.* If we do not grasp this truth, we will not be aware of God's assistance when an enemy appears. While He is trying to tell us what to do, we will be wondering why we are calling for help and no one is answering.

Our enemies may or may not exist in the form of people. If you live in an abusive relationship, there is a person involved, but the real enemy is the abuse, not the person. Fear, sickness, addiction, and memories can also be enemies, but they don't come against us through the life of a person; they are faceless foes. In any case, the rules remain the same. We must face our enemies to defeat them.

I did not want to, but I had to confront abuse. I had to confront fear. I had to confront sickness. I had to confront depression. They were hijackers. They were real. They paralyzed me in their quest to destroy my life. *Only when I faced my hijackers did I truly have any power over them.*

I am not unique in spending a lot of my life not knowing that I needed to face my enemies. Most people have never been taught how to successfully handle conflict. Instead of navigating through it, they hide from it and avoid facing the issues at hand. See if you identify with any of these behaviors regarding conflict:

- You avoid conflict at all costs.

- You talk about the conflict, but not to the person with whom you have the conflict.

- You deal with the stress of conflict by venting about something other than the real issue.

- You divert attention away from the true conflict by arguing about something that feels safe to argue about.

- You get angry or lose your temper in response to conflict as a way to shut down a conversation you don't know how to process.

- You take conflict personally and feel rejected if anyone disagrees with you.

- You focus on the things that are unchangeable such as past decisions or events or other people as a way to avoid dealing with what you do have control over.

- You find it difficult to express what you think or feel.

All of these behaviors can open a door to captivity because in every case, you avoid facing conflict.

Most victims avoid confronting anything in life. To them, confrontation means expressing anger. That's not accurate. *When we confront things, then we are able to let them go.* When we confront things, we are able to move on. I can't move on from my own issues until I confront them, because the only way around them is through. Confrontation is good, because once I've talked to a person about whatever is concerning me or bothering me, then I am released from it. As long as I refuse to confront, I'm caught. Confrontation also releases me to make decisions. It moves me from wondering about things to knowing the truth about things, and once I have the knowledge I need, I can decide what to do about whatever I am confronting. This knowledge should motivate us to confront things often. Again, it is not about anger. There does not need to be any emotion involved at all. There simply needs to be communication on whatever the issue is.

Conflict is not something to be avoided. It can simply be the interaction that takes place when we have a difference of opinion. Conflict does not mean one person is right and the other person is wrong; it just means there are differences. It does not need to threaten or hurt either party; it is just an ordinary part of life. Communication has to continue until there is resolution or agreement. If you can learn to successfully deal with conflict, it will give you a good foundation for dealing with the enemies in your life. When an enemy appears, you will know exactly what to do— you will face it.

Our lives are full of relationships and situations that have a lot of history, and we have to take our new thinking into old situations. One of the biggest challenges I faced in finding freedom was continuing to have to interact with my former husband. It would have been far easier if I could have just dealt with people who did not know the old me, but that was not possible. I had to interact with him on a regular basis because he had custody of our son. I had recognized that I needed to face the situation rather than avoid it, but it was not going very well.

The communication pattern we had established when we were married continued after we were divorced. Shortly into any conversation, there would be an accusation. Generally, the thought of what I was being accused of had never even entered my mind. Thus would begin the crazy ride of a conversation that I never knew how to get off of. I never knew how long it would last or how out of control it was going to get; but it was the only way I could see my son, so each time I went along for the ride.

I responded the only way I knew how—defending and explaining. As soon as I addressed an accusation that he made, he came at me with another one. Confused, I would follow along, trying to bring understanding. The conversation continued from one accusation to the next, always going nowhere and taking the long way to get there. There was never any point and never any conclusion, just inflicted pain from sharp cutting words that sliced to the very core of who I was. It left me feeling exhausted and punished. Facing things was not resolving things for me. Other than giving up and letting go of my relationship with my son, I did not know any way to stop this crazy cycle. Time after time, whenever I called to ask for permission to see my son, I endured. No matter how I tried to prepare myself and stay calm, my heart would race and my palms would sweat. I would find myself unable to think and struggling to speak, paralyzed by the adrenalin coursing through my body in response to the fear I felt.

It was a pattern I could not break on my own. I tried. When I reached the point where I felt I could not endure any more, I asked for help from a friend who I knew did not think the way I did.

Through role playing, we rehearsed an imaginary conversation together. She pretended she was me, and I pretended I was my former husband. Every time she said something, I would come at her with the response I was familiar with, from years of experience. I was shocked at how she approached the situation. She didn't just face it. She made her request, and when accusation was hurled back at her, she stood her ground. She did not defend herself or try to explain; she simply stated truth. No matter what I said to her, she maintained her position of stating the truth and making her request. Over and over again, she stood her ground.

As a victim, I thought I was obligated to defend myself. I thought that if I could make peace, a resolution could be reached. I was caught in a power struggle where I felt like I had to make the other party understand my perspective. But not everyone wants resolution. As long as I responded by defending myself, I was going to lose. I don't mean lose in the sense of there being a winner and a loser. I mean lose in the sense of feeling abused by every conversation and ending up emotionally drained and exhausted. I simply did not know how to stand my ground!

I wrote my friend's words out on a piece of paper in preparation for the next conversation, because I did not trust my memory to be strong enough to override the adrenalin rush that would paralyze me as the dialogue began. I did not have a lot of confidence, but I was willing to try a different approach. It was hard, but I determined that hard with a possible resolution was a better choice than hard with no end in sight. *Never let difficulty stop you if it will achieve the desired result.*

I made the call, and for the first time ever in that relationship, I stood my ground. I made my request. I waited for the accusation. And it came, but it was okay. I did not issue a statement of defense. I simply replied with a statement of truth regarding the real issue and then repeated my request. It took all of my strength to hold my course, but I did it! It felt like I was holding the steering wheel of a vehicle traveling at an out-of-control speed. It seemed by his response that he did not know what to do with me. There was still anger. There was still accusation. There were several attempts to get me to participate in reading the same script that we had read over and over together so many times in our lives. But because I stood my ground, I could not be led into that place of paralysis and pain that was so familiar. When I hung up the phone, it felt completely different from all other conversations. It still wasn't pleasant, but I was free. In standing my ground, I refused to allow someone else's words to hijack my emotions or my thoughts. It was a new day.

Was it a complete victory? It was the beginning of one. The next conversation was difficult but not nearly to the same degree. The one after that was simply tense. The old pattern never repeated between us again, all as a result of my facing the situation and standing my ground. I totally believe in seeking peace. I believe in communication. But if you encounter a situation where resolution is not the goal and you are impaled by another person's words, you cannot respond the same way. If their aim is to hurt and to control, you must shield yourself by holding your position. No matter what, you must refuse to move. *Just because the words are spoken does not mean you have to respond to them.* You are not anyone's slave. You can hear the words and completely disempower them by simply refusing to react.

Stand your ground and state your case. You may have to say things that you've never said before, like, "What you did was wrong." You may need to keep saying it; that is how you maintain control of the situation. Your goal is not to control the other person; your goal is to be in control of your own response. It might feel awkward, but if you stop responding the same way you always have, eventually, you will get a new result.

Don't be afraid to ask for help. If you have never seen another way to respond to a difficult situation than the one you know, it is hard to think one up on your own. The only action you know may be a *reaction*. A reaction is when you re-act out something you have seen someone do or you've already done. Rather than responding, you act as though you have been handed the script of a play and told what lines to read. No matter how the other characters in the play act, you keep reading the same lines over and over again! Reaction halts the thinking process and pushes a button that activates a practiced mode of behavior, causing you to live out the past regardless of what is happening in the present. It puts the situation in charge of you rather than you in charge of the situation.

When you see a parent screaming at a child in a grocery store because the child spilled something, the parent is usually reacting. The behavior does not make sense nor does it clean up the mess. But the parent has been taken hostage by a way of thinking, and is likely *re-acting out* what his or her own parents did, without any thought of responding rather than re-acting.

When my son was about seven, a pattern began to form in his behavior. When he would arrive to spend a weekend with me, he would immediately head downstairs to our unfinished basement where he would put on his rollerblades, grab a stick, and begin to blade around the room. As he neared the steel support beams on each end of the room, he would hit them with his stick, making a loud banging sound that resonated through the entire house. Anger that he was feeling on the inside was being released through hitting something on the outside.

At first, I did not think much about what was happening, but as the banging continued, I would find myself getting angry in response. As my emotions intensified, I would reach a breaking point where I would run downstairs and burst out in anger, commanding him to stop. He was always compliant, but the same behavior would repeat itself the next day or the next visit. One day, in the midst of one of my outbursts, I thought to myself, *Why am I feeling angry?* I was not actually mad about anything; I just wanted the noise to stop. As I recognized that my behavior wasn't making sense, and took time to evaluate it, I realized I was reacting. As I was feeling the anger coming off of my son, I in turn was re-acting out what he was doing. He was acting angry; I was re-acting it. I had been allowing the anger to take control of me. I recognized that I could ask him to stop without getting angry, and so I did. From that point on, I was able to respond instead of react to situations and simply direct what needed to happen.

Victims, people whose lives have been taken hostage, react. Other people respond. That means in every situation we have the ability to think, evaluate, and act in a way that makes sense. It is time to face your enemy and stand your ground.

THINK ABOUT IT

houghts are the seeds of our lives. Rejection doesn't happen because someone calls us a name or leaves us out; it begins with what we think about that experience. Murder doesn't happen because someone picks up a gun; it begins with a thought. Adultery doesn't happen because two people are alone together; it begins with a thought. Most of what we are experiencing in our day-to-day lives reflects what we have been meditating on. What goes on in our minds has more power over our days than anything else. What we think can literally become a life sentence. Proverbs 23:7 says, *"For as he thinks in his heart, so is he…"* (NKJV). I have already explained that it was my thinking, not a person, that enabled abuse to capture me. If we have been hijacked by something, our thinking has to change in order for us to live lives of freedom.

The first step in changing our thinking pattern is to let go of our old ways, the ones we are familiar with. *"Let the wicked forsake their ways, and the unrighteous their thoughts. Let them turn to the Lord…"* (Isaiah 55:7 NIV). Clearly, if the unrighteous and the wicked can forsake their ways and their thoughts, so can everyone else. When I realized that my old way of thinking was my enemy, I decided to leave it behind for good. I was forsaking it, just like the Bible said I should.

It is not enough to tell yourself not to think this or that because you can't just not think. If all we do is try to stop thinking in a negative manner, we will just invite more of the same kind of thoughts. If we are told not to think about something like a snow-storm or an elephant, an image of that thing probably pops right into our heads. Trying not to think about something just doesn't work.

The Bible teaches a principle regarding what happens when we clean something out but don't fill it up: *"When a defiling evil spirit is expelled from someone, it drifts along through the desert looking for an oasis, some unsuspecting soul it can bedevil. When it doesn't find anyone, it says 'I'll go back to my old haunt.' On return it finds the person spot-lessly clean, but vacant. It then runs out and rounds up seven other spirits more evil than itself and they all move in, whooping it up. That person ends up far worse off than if he'd never gotten cleaned up in the first place. That's what this generation is like: You may think you have cleaned out the junk from your lives and gotten ready for God, but you weren't hos-pitable to my kingdom message, and now all the devils are moving back in"* (Matthew 12:43-45 MSG).

Our old way of thinking *must* be replaced with something new. If it isn't, we will end up with even more of the same thoughts. When we let go of one way of thinking and embrace a new one, we change our life sentence. We were living out one way of thinking, one life sentence, but we can change our thoughts and change our lives.

How can we replace our old way of thinking with a new one? In seeking the answer to that question, I discovered that God has a way of thinking: *"For my thoughts are not your thoughts, neither are your ways my ways," declares the Lord. "As the heavens are higher than the earth, so are my ways higher than your ways and my thoughts than your thoughts"* (Isaiah 55:8-9 NIV).

Scripture reveals what that way of thinking is: *"Finally, brothers and sisters, whatever is true, whatever is noble, whatever is right, what-ever is pure, whatever is lovely, whatever is admirable—if anything is ex-cellent or praiseworthy—think about such things"* (Philippians 4:8 NIV). In order to produce God-results in my life, I would have to think God-thoughts in my mind. The concept of thought bound-aries were a revelation to me. I had to ask myself why I would give myself permission to think about certain things. I wouldn't meditate on murder, adultery, or lust, so why would I meditate on rejection, fear, or worry? It was the beginning of a new way of life. In changing my thinking, I was changing my life sentence.

I began to use Philippians 4:8 as a way to monitor my thoughts to see if I was thinking in a godly (life-giving) way or a destructive way. I wrote the verse on a sticky-note and put it on my bathroom mirror where it would capture my attention each day. When I saw it, I would take a moment and evaluate what I was thinking about. Was it true? Pure? Lovely? Praiseworthy? Generally, it wasn't. More often, my thoughts were negative, fearful, and hopeless. And so I would tell myself, "You don't have the right to think this way." Sometimes I would actually speak out loud as I stood there, saying, "I am forsaking these thoughts. I refuse to give any more life to them." In fighting to establish a new pattern of thinking, I was fighting for my life.

Philippians 4:8 also became a weapon I used to defend my new way of thinking, because I knew *my life would only change as much as my thoughts did.* I couldn't afford to be a victim anymore! Day after day, week after week, I was setting a new pattern. The more I consciously lined up my thinking with what was true, lovely, pure, and admirable, the more naturally my thoughts began to flow that way. I was becoming a new person, living a different kind of life, because *I thought so.*

Another way I protected my new way of thinking was by choosing to cut out any influences that reinforced what I used to believe about myself and about life. I eliminated books and shows such as soap operas that I once enjoyed, realizing they would strengthen the very thoughts I was trying to leave behind. Soap operas and the kinds of books I read were filled with stories of people living as the victims of other people's actions. They only have two kinds of characters: perpetrators and victims. I enjoyed the stories because they made me feel like I wasn't alone; I could identify with the characters who were feeling the same kind of pain I was. I realized that I couldn't expose myself to that kind of content without spiraling downward again. The shows or books would seem enjoyable at the time, but then the old familiar thoughts would come flooding back. My decision was not about whether a show or book was good or bad; it was about whether it brought freedom or captivity to me.

As I continued to work to change my mindset, I recognized that I could not learn everything I needed to on my own. It was necessary to find people who were healthy in the areas of life I was struggling in and learn from them how to *think about it.* I watched, listened, and asked them questions. I asked what they would think or do in certain situations. I asked how they would respond to certain events. Often they gave me answers that I had never imagined before. Sometimes their answers were so foreign to me that I would have to make notes that I could refer back to because I couldn't grasp it all at once. My whole mind was changing. It was empowering and fascinating to be able to change in a way I hadn't even known was possible.

We are in a battle for our thoughts because how we think about things determines how they will be. Second Corinthians 10:4-5 says, *"The weapons we fight with are not the weapons of the world. On the contrary, they have divine power to demolish strongholds. We demolish arguments and every pretension that sets itself up against the knowledge of God, and we take captive every thought to make it obedient to Christ"* (NIV).

Every day was a battle for me. I was plagued by thoughts of guilt about my past. I had been accused of so many things that when I would go to my son's kindergarten class to be a parent helper or to the hockey rink to cheer him on at one of his games, I felt like I had a huge sign on my forehead that said *freak.* I was sure that everyone had been told lies about me, and I was tormented over what people thought about me the entire time I was there. It was only my love for my son and wanting to be there for him that enabled me to endure the war in my mind.

The more control a certain kind of thinking had on me in the past, the more of a battle it took to completely defeat it. Thinking I was rejected was a huge stronghold I had to tear down. I clearly remember the first time I attended a women's conference. I had been excited about going, but as I approached the registration table, I was assaulted by thoughts I didn't anticipate. Rejection launched an all-out attack with thoughts like, *What are you doing here? There's nothing here for you. Who do you think you are? You'd better leave now before anyone notices.* It took everything in me to hold my ground and not walk back out the door.

Thinking I needed a drink when life got pressured was a thought that visited me for years. I never acted on that thought, but it was vigilant to knock on my door time after time, checking to see if *today* might be the day I would invite it in and entertain it. When I reflect on some of my family members who struggled with alcohol addiction, I wonder how many of them were visited by that same thought.

My thinking patterns did not change overnight. It required perseverance, practice, and time. Thoughts would still regularly come my way that I would recognize as wrong. Sometimes those kinds of thoughts still come. I cannot control that. But I have complete control over whether or not I let those thoughts occupy my mind. I don't have to let someone in my house just because they knock on my door; in the same way, I don't have to entertain a thought just because it comes into my head.

Our thought patterns are primarily passed on to us from our family. When those thoughts patterns are outside of God's ways, dysfunction or destruction will result. That does not mean that the symptoms of the dysfunction will manifest in every family member, but it does mean that a dysfunctional system of thought will usually permeate the whole family. For instance, in a family where there is a stronghold of thinking that eventually produces the symptom of alcoholism, not every family member will be an alcoholic. However, every family member will contribute to the dysfunction by the way they think. These people are called enablers. They don't manifest the symptoms themselves, but they enable the family member who does. If it wasn't this way, people could get free from dysfunction simply by leaving home. That seldom happens because when a person leaves home, they take their pattern of thinking with them.

When one person in a family decides to change their thinking and takes a stand against abuse, alcoholism, poverty, or some other

I DON'T THINK SO

type of hijacker, it usually throws the entire family into chaos. Since they all participate through their stronghold of thinking, they will often rise to the defense of that stronghold, not even recognizing what they are doing. Typically, they will come against the person trying to get free because of their own fear and victim mentality. If they aren't ready to confront the stronghold themselves, they will try to get everyone to go back to normal—however abnormal that may be. That's why a victim of sexual abuse can come forward and end up being the one blamed by the family for the abuse. That's why an alcoholic can try to stop drinking and someone in the family encourages them with "just a glass of wine." Everyone in the family is a victim because of how they think, and each one has to change their own way of thinking in order to get free.

If you are making the decision to change your thinking, evaluate the people surrounding you to determine if they, too, are hijacked by a wrong way of thinking. If they are, it is unlikely they will be able to help you on your journey to freedom. They may react negatively as you begin to make different choices. Do not expect everyone to understand you; they won't. Find a couple of people you trust and let them support you through the process. Beyond them, keep your information to yourself as much as possible. There will be plenty of time to share truth when you have won the battle.

As my thought patterns changed and I began to experience a different quality of life, I sometimes had thoughts that I just could not resolve. For instance, I had an experience where a previous boss wrongly judged my motives in doing something. Although I did not feel like I was guilty of what he had accused me of, I somehow could not get past it. The situation would play over and over again in my mind, and I was unable to bring it to a point of closure. What was the glue that was causing this thought to stick to me when I wanted it gone? I discovered it was doubt. *Doubt creates instability in our thinking.* It keeps us from moving forward in a productive way because we keep changing the direction of our thoughts. I didn't think I was guilty, but then I would doubt it. So I wavered back and forth.

Scripture describes this process clearly: "...*you must believe and not doubt, because the one who doubts is like a wave of the sea, blown and tossed by the wind. ....Such a person is double-minded and unstable in all they do"* (James 1:6,8 NIV). I realized that if my boss had accused me of something that I didn't have any doubt about, his words would not have been able to have any power over me. I would have been able to conclude that he was wrong and move on. But when I wasn't sure whether I was guilty or not, doubt captured me. Now when I find myself caught in waves of double-mindedness about something, I recognize that it is a sign of doubt. I examine what it is I have doubt about, and work toward establishing the truth. Once I know the truth, I can move forward.

The life you are living is the life you are thinking. No one else can force you to think anything. Since you are in charge of your thoughts, if you want to change your thinking, you can. Tomorrow doesn't have to look like yesterday. Let go of your old ways. Fill your thoughts with what is true, lovely, and praiseworthy. Fight the battle until you win. Keep a vigilant watch over what you let in to your mind. What is the life that you want to live? It's in your power to think about it.

You will keep in perfect peace all who trust in you, all whose thoughts are fixed on you! (Isaiah 26:3)

Chapter 17

THE POWER OF FORGIVENESS

Forgiveness is a powerful tool designed to protect us from captivity. Like any weapon, forgiveness is only useful when we understand how to use it. Since there are a lot of misconceptions about what forgiveness really is, there are a lot of people with no idea how to effectively put it to work in their lives. Many believe that forgiveness is wearing a brave face and pretending that wounds do not hurt. This is especially true in the Christian world where we have been taught over and over again that we *must* forgive. When we don't know what that really means, we fake it because we would not want to be found guilty of unforgiveness. When someone apologizes to us, we cover our lack of understanding by responding, "Oh, that's okay," or "It was nothing."

If you have been hurt, rejected, insulted, abandoned, or abused, God will never tell you that it was nothing. He will not say that you don't have a right to be hurt or that what happened was okay. If those things had been okay, then Jesus would not have had to suffer them. Isaiah 53:3 says that He was *"despised and rejected by men, a Man of sorrows and acquainted with grief..."* (NKJV). In other words, Jesus suffered so that we would not have to become imprisoned by pain. Although God will not tell you it was okay, He will tell you to forgive because forgiveness is the process God designed to deal with hurt.

What does *forgive* mean? It means that you acknowledge that there has been an offense, you acknowledge the cost of that offense, and you choose to let Jesus cover the cost. You allow Him to pay the bill. You move the offender out of the courtroom of your heart and into God's courtroom. Forgiveness transfers the debt and the burden of that debt from you to Him.

The truth is no one can ever repay you for cheating you, hurting you, abandoning you, rejecting you, or abusing you. At best, they can be sorry, but they cannot repay you because they cannot undo what they have done. Think about it. If someone stepped on your toes, it would hurt. There would be an *offense*. If they were sorry for doing it, they could apologize, but the bottom line is that there is no way that they can un-step on your toes and no way that they can stop the pain they caused. The same is true with any kind of offense. Words cannot be retracted, events cannot be relived, and time cannot be turned back. *Offense cannot be undone.*

When you hold someone in unforgiveness, refusing to let go of the offense committed against you, you are literally trying to collect a bill that can never be paid. In effect, you have decided that someone owes you and you are always trying to collect. Offense is a black hole that continually demands payment. It does not matter how much people do for you or how much they try to make it up to you, *unless you forgive, you will be the prisoner of that offense for the rest of your life.*

So how does forgiveness really work? Imagine that I invite you out for lunch and tell you that I am going to pay for your meal. You place your order and enjoy your food. At the end of the meal you are presented with the bill. That bill acknowledges your debt, what you owe, or the cost that was just incurred. We both know what was ordered, we both know what the cost was, but I pay the bill and you do nothing except receive my gift. In allowing me to take responsibility for the bill, you don't hide it, sweep it under the rug, or pretend you didn't eat anything. Instead, you say, "Here is my debt; here is the cost of it." Then you let me take responsibility for that debt and pay for it. What happens is a transfer of responsibility; it is not pretending you did not order any lunch. You certainly do not say, "It was nothing."

When someone hurts you, saying it was nothing, is like pretending you did not order any lunch. This accomplishes nothing. It creates toxicity in your heart, because on the outside you deny its existence, but on the inside you believe you are owed a debt. This is true even if you know the person did not intend to hurt you. Motive is irrelevant. *You can never be healed from a hurt by saying it was okay. Forgiveness is the only weapon with the power to free you.*

Think about the people you need to forgive. Who sends off a high octane ping in your senses when you think about them or hear their name? Who is it that you think owes you? Who has the power to cause your whole body to react if they were to enter the room right now? Name them. Identify who it is that owes you.

Now name what the offense was. Perhaps it was betrayal, abandonment, sarcasm, rejection, abuse, or humiliation. Call it what it was. Name it. It may make you uncomfortable to do this exercise, but if you cannot name it, then it does not exist. If it does not exist, then you cannot forgive it because there is nothing to forgive so you stay trapped.

Once you have named the offense, determine its cost. Just like a meal has a cost, so does an offense. It will generally be identified in the context of a feeling such as it hurt or it made me feel worthless, foolish, betrayed, terrified, unlovable, etc. Why is this necessary? It is just like the bill for your meal—you cannot do anything about it until you know what the bill was for and what it cost.

Now choose to let Jesus cover the cost. Let Him take responsibility for it. Let Him pay for it. That was His purpose in subjecting Himself to the suffering He went through. How do you let Him cover the cost? Through prayer. "Lord, here is what this person did to me. Here is their debt. And here is what it cost me. I can never collect this debt. It cannot be undone. But You paid the price with Your life so that this debt might not rule over me. I choose to take this person out of the courtroom of my heart, and I place him or her into Your courtroom, for You are the One true judge. I am allowing You to pay the bill, and I forgive the person. I cancel the debt, and I declare that the person owes me nothing."

You are not saying what the person did to you was okay and you are not saying that what he or she did was nothing. You are transferring responsibility for dealing with the matter from you to God. You are releasing yourself from a debt that can never be paid, only cancelled. You are releasing yourself from an otherwise lifelong sentence. You are doing what we should always do with anything toxic—get rid of it as quickly as possible. You are taking the way of escape that God has provided. It has nothing to do with the person you are forgiving; it is all for you! *Forgiveness is a weapon you cannot live without.*

Several years ago, someone hurt me very badly. Even though the person knew that the behavior was wrong and that it was causing me great pain, the person chose to do it anyway. I became deeply offended. I found myself complaining about this person over and over to God. Day after day, I would rehearse how hurt I was and how wrong the person was and how much was owed me. Clearly God was not hearing me because the situation did not change; and instead of getting better, the pain in my heart got worse. The more I complained, the more it bothered me, and the more it bothered me, the more I complained.

One day at lunch time, alone in my car, I began my usual rant to God about the situation. Before I could finish the first sentence, God interrupted me. In my mind, I clearly heard these words, "I died for that person's sin, so what do you have to say about it?" I was shocked. I felt as though I had been slapped across the face. Truth brought me to my senses and caused me to realize that God had not been ignoring me and was not oblivious to my pain. In fact, He was telling me that He fully knew the pain I had suffered as a result of this person's sin, and He had paid the penalty for it Himself so I could be free. There was nothing more He could do; He had fully cancelled the debt. Now it was up to me to forgive. I let go of my offense then and there, realizing that what had happened could never be undone, only forgiven. In forgiving, I was released from the pain that had tormented me for months. Although that person's behavior never changed, its power over me was broken. Once I had forgiven, I was free to be in the person's presence and be unaffected by the behavior. *Forgiveness released me from captivity.*

If you are reading this and thinking, *But I don't have anything to forgive,* then I encourage you to take another look and be real with yourself. I have never met anyone who has not experienced some kind of hurt in their life. If you have processed hurt by denying that it exists, it is like a ticking time bomb inside of you that will eventually go off. I say this because I have walked side by side with people (who seemed to be following Christ the same way I was) who chose to sidestep the issue of forgiveness. When they were given the opportunity to forgive, they chose instead to say, "It was nothing." As time passed, that decision proved to be a fork in the road that eventually separated them from God and from others who loved them. I watched as the offenses that they denied ate away at their lives. *By refusing to forgive, they bound themselves to the hurt and allowed it to rule over them long after it had ended.* I urge you not to let another day go by without forgiving. Take the time necessary to identify all the offenses you have been living with—then take the time to pray through each one.

⊹═⊹═⊹═⊹

Not only is it necessary to forgive others, we must forgive ourselves for our own sins and failures. Sometimes the person we need to forgive the most is ourselves. You may have been diligent in allowing God to take care of the debts of others, but never allowed Him to take the burden of your debts. Consider the following questions:

- What is it that you need to forgive yourself for?

- What have you done that makes you sick when you think about it?

- What do you regret? What do you beat yourself up over?

- What mistake did you make or what did you fail to do?

- What holds you in depression or grief?

- What completes the sentence, "If only I hadn't _____"?

No voice can stop people in their tracks faster than the voice of guilt. Fear can paralyze us, but the voice of guilt is accompanied by the hopelessness that comes from knowing that there is no way to undo whatever it is we feel guilty about. If there was a way to undo it, we would have done it. Guilt resides in the deep underground of our consciences, biding its time in silence as it waits for the moment of opportunity to present itself. It might be the opportunity to begin a new relationship, the opportunity for a promotion, or the opportunity for some kind of advancement. The door swings open, beckoning us in, and our hearts beat faster at the prospect of what has just opened up for us. Initially, waves of excitement and possibility sweep over us, but then out of nowhere a rogue wave of guilt picks us up off our feet and sweeps us into the bottomless memory of some failure, mistake, or shortcoming of which we are guilty. We are caught in the bittersweet turmoil of our hearts eagerly longing for what we see before us and condemning us for what is behind. We are unable to embrace what lies ahead because we do not know how to escape from past failure. Since we know that we are guilty, we feel that we have no choice but to act condemned. Opportunity passes on by, and those around us wonder what happened and why we did not lay hold of it.

The experience of guilt is not unique; it is the result of the disease of sin that infects everyone. In fact, the Bible teaches in Romans 3:23 that, *"all have sinned and fall short of the glory of God"* (NIV). In other words, all of us have areas of failure and have been unable to live up to the standard we set for ourselves. That is no secret. But what seems to be hidden to most people is what to do about it. The Bible does not keep it secret; it is plainly written for us to understand: *"Yet God, with undeserved kindness, declares that we are righteous. He did this through Christ Jesus when he freed us from the penalty for our sins. For God presented Jesus as the sacrifice for sin. People are made right with God when they believe that Jesus sacrificed his life, shedding his blood..."* (Romans 3:24-25). The process of forgiveness is not complete until you have released yourself from your own failures.

As far as God is concerned, if we have received Jesus' gift of forgiveness, then our record has been wiped clean. But this cleansing requires us to forgive ourselves in the same way we have already talked about forgiving others. Just as other people are unable to undo the offenses they have committed against us, we are unable to undo the offenses we have committed. The same weapon of forgiveness that frees us from the offenses of others will free us from our own guilt. We must forgive ourselves in order to silence the voice of guilt and be free to embrace the life ahead of us. *Forgiveness does not deny the guilt; it gives us the power to face our failure and move past it.*

You can do that by praying a prayer like this: "Lord, today, I forgive myself for my failure. I allow You to pay the price for all that I did wrong. I release myself from the courtroom of my heart, from my self-judgment, self-loathing, and self-condemnation. I cannot undo the past, so I acknowledge the cost today, and I transfer the responsibility of this debt to You. I choose to let You pay the price for my failure. As you have forgiven me, I forgive myself." Once you have forgiven yourself, your confidence will grow because you know that your debt has been paid.

If you find yourself in a relationship where a person continually hurts you, it is more difficult to keep forgiving—but you can do it. You might have dealt with the offense and removed it from your heart, but then they hurt you again. You have to start over. Clearly this happened to Peter in the Bible because he said to Jesus, *"Lord, how often shall my brother sin against me, and I forgive him? Up to seven times?" Jesus said to him, "I do not say to you, up to seven times, but up to seventy times seven"* (Matthew 18:21-22 NKJV). Jesus was saying you need to forgive as often as you are offended because forgiveness is what brings freedom. How many times do you have to wash your car? As many times as you want it clean. How many times do you have to forgive? As many times as you want to remain free. What would be the point in forgiving seven times and being ensnared the eighth time?

Forgiveness is a weapon given to us to continually wield against the offenses that come. Wield it well and often! *Fight valiantly for your freedom.* It is yours for the taking. Be diligent to practice forgiveness for the rest of your life. We live in a broken world where there will always be opportunities to be hurt. Forgiveness is a most powerful weapon!

In this manner, therefore, pray: Our Father in heaven, hallowed be Your name. Your kingdom come. Your will be done on earth as it is in heaven. Give us this day our daily bread. And forgive us our debts, as we forgive our debtors. And do not lead us into temptation, but deliver us from the evil one. For Yours is the kingdom and the power and the glory forever. Amen (Matthew 6:9-13 NKJV).

Chapter 18

SECRETS

He was a good man. He lived a good life. He left home when he was still a boy, looking for the opportunity to prove himself. He worked hard to make his way in life and was always a good provider. A caring and loving husband, father, and grandfather, he lived a generous life, freely sharing what he had. He stood up for what he believed in, and he wasn't afraid to take a stand. He had many friends, and he was deeply loved. But a cloud of darkness followed the man throughout his life. Depression would sneak up seemingly from nowhere. It would settle in like a thick fog, obscuring all hope and taking him hostage. He could not see past it and all the words in the world could not clear it out. He was caught in its grip. Then it would leave as suddenly as it had come, and life would go on peaceably for a time. In the same way that the sun shines after a storm has passed, life was good when the cloud lifted. Inevitably, it would return without warning, blocking out all light and hope, and leaving its mark on him and everyone around him.

The darkness didn't just mark him; it marked some of his siblings. You could see it on their faces. It was as if they had seen something horrific and could not get the image out of their minds. It was a darkness and sorrow they could not escape, a pain they couldn't ease, and a fear they couldn't squelch. To those observing, it was just a heavy cloud that no one talked about and could never be named, but everyone knew it was there. Some of the siblings coped with alcohol. Some coped with drugs. Some coped with rage. And some could not cope at all and chose to take their own lives. They were hijacked, not by the cloud of depression, but by the secrets that hid behind it.

The darkness tormented the man all of his life. Not only the darkness of his past, but fear of it arising in the next generation or the next. He lived in fear of it and tried to control everything as a means of protecting his family from it, but his struggle was futile. There was nowhere he could go to get away from it. He did his best to live a good life, but the past haunted him. As he neared the end of his days, the power of depression intensified and life became unbearable. And then one day, the man saw a vision. He saw a book with his name written in it, and underneath his name was a list of all his sins. In that moment of realization, he knew that he could no longer hold it in. Like a volcano, it all came spilling out, the collection of secrets from his childhood that had haunted him for most of his life. The pressure of holding it in all those years was too much, and the words began pouring out. He had to tell and he had to tell all of it, regardless of what anyone thought.

No one knew what to say, but it didn't matter to him. He had found freedom. The vision brought the realization that the secrets weren't really secrets—God knew it all. The Bible says that one day we will give an account (see Hebrews 4:13), and God will bring our darkest secrets to light and will reveal our private motives (see 1 Corinthians 4:5). The man's secrets had hijacked his life, and he knew that their power would be destroyed when he gave them up. So he confessed. For the first time in his life, he was free from the torment of the secrets. The hijacking was over and peace flooded in. The darkness would own him no more. The Amplified version of Ephesians 5:13 says, *"But when anything is exposed and reproved by the light, it is made visible and clear; and where everything is visible and clear there is light."* Now the cloud of depression and endless fear all made sense. His family had not known that it was the secrets that had really tormented him. The depression they had repeatedly tried to talk him out of was only a symptom caused by isolation and shame.

Secrets cause people to think they are the only ones who have ever done such a thing. There are many kinds of secrets that hold people captive. One of the most common hijackers is secrets that involve sexual sin. Sexual secrets are not new; they are a trap described in the Bible. Proverbs 7:21-23 says, *"With much justifying and enticing argument she persuades him, with the allurements of her lips she leads him [to overcome his conscience and his fears] and forces him along. Suddenly he [yields and] follows her reluctantly like an ox moving to the slaughter, like one in fetters going to the correction [to be given] to a fool or like a dog enticed by food to the muzzle. Till a dart [of passion] pierces and inflames his vitals; then like a bird fluttering straight into the net [he hastens], not knowing that it will cost him his life"* (AMP).

Perhaps you have been hijacked this way. You might not even remember when it began in your life. You may have blocked it out, but it may have happened something like this: You didn't intend for it to happen, and you never realized it would go so far. It began as a thought. At first you were shocked that you could have imagined such a thing. But as you entertained it in the privacy of your own mind, you began to wonder what it would be like. You began to wonder how it would feel. The longer you thought about it and the more times you turned it over in your mind, the more you wanted to know. As you continued to secretly think about it, the want became a need, and the desire grew until one day you acted on it. You made the way for it to happen. The anticipation of the experience coupled with the conviction that it was wrong and the fear of being caught caused your pulse to race and adrenalin to course through your body. You didn't intend to hurt anyone. You just wanted to see. You just wanted to know. You wanted some comfort, something to ease your pain or your loneliness. Something to fill the void. You told yourself it would be okay.

When it was over, an ocean of guilt came crashing in, pounding your soul and leaving you sick at the thought of what you had done. It wasn't okay at all. Like a drug, it took you to the highest high and then cast you down into the deepest, darkest pit, laughing at your foolishness. As it replayed in your mind, your first reaction was denial. You wouldn't have done something like that. Something so appalling couldn't have happened. You told yourself that's not who you are, but at the same time you knew that's what you did. It was almost too much for your mind to process. But it did happen and there was no way to go back, no way to undo it. It was your first secret. *"Then the evil desire, when it has conceived, gives birth to sin, and sin, when it is fully matured, brings forth death"* (James 1:15 AMP).

You struggled to reconcile yourself to knowing you had done something so shameful. A war broke out. The horror of what you had done, the screaming of your conscience, and the realization that you couldn't undo it launched an all-out assault. It demanded retribution but there was none to give, no way to pay it off. The assault went relentlessly on, and your mind and heart screamed in anguish until suddenly you could not hold it together anymore and your mind split into what felt like a million pieces, like a rock shattering a pane of glass. What couldn't be reconciled had to be separated in order to bear it. And you went on with life, keeping everything carefully compartmentalized. If you could just keep the parts from touching one another on the inside, perhaps you could maintain control. So you filed the memory in one place and your conscience in another. You did your best to always only allow an audience of one in your mind at a time because if you invited two, war would break out again. The control was only a farce, because you were not in control at all. The secret now controlled you.

You had regret and remorse. You wished it had never happened. You wished you could go back. When you knew you could not go back, you promised yourself it would never happen again. You searched for a way to get free from the guilt and shame, but it was futile. There was no way out of the prison in which you found yourself. The torment never stopped. The deepest sleep wasn't enough to keep you from waking up to the horrific memory of it all. The longest shower wasn't enough to make you feel clean. There weren't enough tears to wash away the guilt. The strongest drink wasn't enough to overpower it, and the strongest drug wasn't enough to numb it. No matter how many good things you did, you couldn't atone for it.

Days turned into weeks, weeks turned into months, months turned into years. At first, the horror was strong and there was much fear of being found out. But as time passed and the secret went undetected and your soul became numb, you began to guard it vigilantly. Eventually, when the burden of the guilt became too much to bear, you decided that if you were paying the price anyway, you might as well do it again. If there was no way out, you might as well go back for more. After all, it felt good. You enjoyed it, so you acted again. And your secret became secrets. Your collection had begun. Over time it grew. You no longer wondered what it would be like; you now had an appetite for more of it—the ecstasy, the rush, the excitement that momentarily seared your conscience. It hijacked and controlled you. Your life became a web of carefully orchestrated lies that covered your sin. The secrets required your constant attention and monitoring to make sure everything was kept in check. You were forever looking over your shoulder and worrying that you might let something slip. Keeping your tracks covered often meant moving from relationship to relationship or even from city to city.

Sometimes you would vow that a new beginning somewhere would mark the start of freedom for you, but it never did. You could not keep the secrets silent, and eventually they would drive you to act out again. In some seasons it would fade into the background, pretending it had only been a passing fad or a bad choice, but then out of nowhere its appetite would rage again, sending you on a quest to collect one more secret. Your life was not your own.

You found ways to justify it in your mind. You told yourself you had needs. If you took something that didn't belong to you, you told yourself it was love or that they wanted it, enjoyed it or deserved it. It may have made you feel better, or feel good about yourself, but it wasn't given to you; you took it. They may have agreed; but if they did, it was because you tricked or deceived them into giving you what you wanted. You told yourself you weren't hurting anyone. Or maybe you knew you were hurting them but you wanted someone else to feel pain.

No matter what story you told yourself to counteract the guilt, you never quite escaped the torment of the prison where your secrets kept you trapped. Some days, it seemed as though you were two people: the one who carried on a seemingly normal life, and the one who lived in captivity to the secrets. As repulsion and compulsion warred with one another over and over again, the lines of right and wrong became blurred. How far was too far? What was right and what was wrong? When the desire became too strong, you succumbed once again and another secret became yours to keep.

There is a way out. *"Where can I go from Your Spirit? Or where can I flee from Your presence? If I ascend into heaven, You are there; if I make my bed in hell, behold, You are there"* (Psalm 139:7-8 NKJV). That means a secret is really a prison you trap yourself in by refusing to tell. You are not keeping the secret in; you are keeping freedom out. Keeping the secret is not protecting you; you are under its control. Haven't you had enough of the secrets?

Secrets are one of the ugliest hijackers. They are invisible and insidious, operating with puppet strings that jerk and contort people, sometimes for their entire lives. Your secret might not be the kind I described. Perhaps you had an affair or an abortion. Maybe you gave a baby up for adoption or maybe you fathered a child and moved on. Maybe you ran from something you did not know how to face. You may live every day wondering when you wake up if today might be the day your world crashes because someone from your past shows up and reveals your secret. You are tormented at the thought of what people would think if they knew. That is a prison in which you were never intended to live. You could not cope with the secret then, and you don't feel like you can cope with it now. If you are running and cannot stop, you have been hijacked.

I hate secrets as much as I hate fear or abuse or any other hijacker because I hate what they do to people. I remember finding out one summer that a friend's father had had another family. He had another wife and other children, and my friend knew nothing about it. It explained a lot of things about my friend's family. It explained why everything was so regimented in their home and why there were so many things that my friend would not even considering talking to her father about. The strange, no-questions-asked policy in her home was explained when I understood that the father was living hijacked by a secret. He had set up walls to protect the secret, and both of his families paid the price.

Secrets cause people to act strangely. Their behavior is often perceived as bizarre because they are living under the influence of something no one can see. Some live exerting extreme control, holding everything down in an attempt to hide the secret. Others demonstrate no control. Just like the wind, you can see its effects on their lives, but you can never see the source. No one understands what force it is that causes their lives to twist and turn and stir up dust and debris all around them.

The way to be set free from this hijacker is to confess. The thought of that might be horrifying. If people knew, your world could crumble. You could lose your reputation or your job or your friends. The stakes are high. Confession might not seem to be an option at all because of the fear of loss. You do not think you could face those who love you. Your spouse. Your children. You can't imagine the thought of losing them if they turn on you. However, no one truly knows you, so being alone is a reality you are already living. Secrets keep you isolated. Isolation looks for comfort. Comfort creates more secrets. You get caught in an endless cycle. You do not want to hurt the people you love. But you are deceived if you think they aren't paying a price. They live with your anger, your abuse, your control, your depression, or whatever way the secrets manifest in your life. They don't know why you react or what makes you withdraw. The greatest gift you could give them is to set everyone free. Enough is enough. It is time to tell the truth.

"Confess to one another therefore your faults (your slips, your false steps, your offenses, your sins) and pray [also] for one another, that you may be healed and restored [to a spiritual tone of mind and heart]..." (James 5:16 AMP). By confessing, you walk out of the prison and silence all the threats. You end the hijacking and walk away free. You break the power sin has held over you. Jesus died to free you from the secrets. Matthew 10:26-28 says, *"Don't be intimidated. Eventually everything is going to be out in the open, and everyone will know how things really are. So don't hesitate to go public now. Don't be bluffed into silence by the threats of bullies. There's nothing they can do to your soul,*

your core being. Save your fear for God, who holds your entire life—body and soul—in his hands" (MSG).

The first thing to do to get free is to make things right between you and God. You may believe that what you have done stands between you and God, but the truth is that God knows all about what you have done. He is waiting for you to accept the exchange that was made for your sin. He did not die because you got it right; He died because you could not get it right. His blood covers your sin. You have to stop trying to cover it yourself and receive His gift of forgiveness. Instead of trying to clean up the mess, instead of trying to escape from the mess, why not allow Jesus right into the mess? You can't clean it up, but He can. Romans 5:8 says, *"But God demonstrates His own love toward us, in that while we were still sinners, Christ died for us"* (NKJV).

The result of coming to God with your sin is forgiveness. Why not end the separation today? Confess, come clean, and walk into the light. You can pray right now, tell your secrets to Him, and receive His forgiveness. First John 1:9 says, *"If we confess our sins, He is faithful and just to forgive us our sins and to cleanse us from all unrighteousness"* (NKJV). If you are not yet convinced that forgiveness is available, here is another verse for you: *"Now that we know what we have—Jesus, this great High Priest with ready access to God—let's not let it slip through our fingers. We don't have a priest who is out of touch with our reality. He's been through weakness and testing, experienced it all—all but the sin. So let's walk right up to him and get what he is so ready to give. Take the mercy, accept the help"* (Hebrews 4:14-16 MSG).

If you feel it is too much to process alone, then I encourage you to contact a pastor and allow him or her to pray through it with you. The man I spoke of earlier went into eternity knowing he was right with God. You, too, have the opportunity to live from now on in right standing with God.

Once you have made it right with God, you need to establish who you need to tell. This requires wisdom and will depend what the secrets are and when they happened. Were you a child or an adult when they happened? Were other people involved? Were they children or adults? Was trust broken? Was a covenant broken? Was a crime committed? Do you owe someone something? Can restitution be made? *Take some time to think through these things and get a proper perspective and a plan before you act*—or you could cause unnecessary crisis because you were only thinking of yourself. When you have been holding something in for so long, once a decision is made to come forth, the pressure to just get it all out in the open can override common sense.

Again, I caution you to think it through and choose the wisest way to reveal everything. If the confession will cause others pain, it will get worse before it gets better. Breaking free from any hijacker is a messy process. I suggest that you find a trusted friend, pastor, or counselor who can help you walk through it. Having the advice, wisdom, and perspective of an outside party could be invaluable in helping everyone involved.

The secrets you hold may have happened a long time ago and not affect anyone in your present world. You have to ask yourself if it will help anyone to know. In this situation, making it right with God may be sufficient action for you to move on. Once you have received His forgiveness, you may be able to embrace life fully and no one else necessarily needs to know. Do not tell others if the only result will be that you feel better. There is no reason to bring them unnecessary pain.

If the secrets have broken trust or covenants with people in your life today, the truth has to be told in order for the destruction of the secret to be stopped in those relationships. If you have committed adultery, you cannot move forward in your marriage without there being repentance and forgiveness. It is likely that you will need the help of a pastor or counselor to help you work through this, and it will take some time. If you have children, their ages will determine whether or not they are included in the process. It would be unfair for young children to be told things they lack the maturity to understand; but if they are old enough, they need to be included in the process for healing to flow to the entire family. In general, you need to work from the inside out, talking to those closest to you first. Because your spouse and family are the most valuable relationships you have, they are the place where you have the most to lose if they cannot forgive you. Every situation is unique, and I encourage you to use wisdom and talk your plan through with a trusted person before you proceed.

If there are people to whom you owe restitution, that is the next step. Do what you need to do to make it right. Write a letter of apology. Start by saying that you are sorry. Then take responsibility for what you did. It will probably be a process. Perhaps you robbed someone of something. Perhaps you have a child you turned your back on physically, emotionally, and financially. You can't make up for lost time, but you can use the time you have. Start contributing today.

What if you have committed a crime? It is one thing to confess that you have some sort of addiction, another thing to confess adultery, but something else entirely to confess a crime. The nature of some secrets could have legal consequences. You may be caught in this scenario thinking, "If I tell, I will pay. If I tell, they will lock me up." You feel you can't come forward because of the potential consequences. The truth is you are already imprisoned. If you keep the secret, you remain a prisoner forever; but you will experience freedom by taking responsibility and facing the consequences of your actions. No one will hold anything over you anymore. No ghosts will haunt you. The consequences can actually bring the healing and wholeness that have evaded you.

Be aware that if you have committed a crime and you turn to someone for help with the process of coming clean, you may obligate the person you tell to go to the police. Do not let that deter you; instead, do it in such a way that you do not put them in that position. Once you have made a decision to take responsibility for your actions, prepare the person you are about to confide in. Tell them you would like their help to face something from the past that may have legal consequences. Outline what is about to happen before you give them the facts. They can help you make a plan if you restrict what you tell them to the nature of the situation, as opposed to the facts of the situation, until you are ready to move forward. You can put the person in a position to help by telling them that you already know there will be consequences. It may be wise to seek the advice of a lawyer. Decide to get free, and access the help you need to process the truth.

Do not be held captive by the fear of what you might lose. Your decision may be costly in terms of relationships, financial position, or even physical freedom, but none of those compare with the freedom of your soul. God can take what the enemy intends for evil in your life and turn it for good, but secrets will always be destructive. They will keep all your relationships at a superficial level. They will keep you looking over your shoulder wondering if anyone knows. They will keep you in guilt and torment. There is great freedom in telling the truth. Once you have confessed, the threats will be silenced. All of their ammunition will be gone. The power of secrets that held you captive, making you unable to be who you really are, will be broken. Freedom is so much better than the captivity in which you have been living.

When you tell the truth, there is no guarantee that the people you tell will respond as you hope or expect. Not everyone will understand and forgive. I can't tell you that you won't lose anyone in the process. I think about the pastor who molested me so long ago and what the cost would be in his life if he were to confess. It could be very high. However, every day he lives in silence is another day he is hijacked by the secret. I am not bound by that secret because I forgave him long ago. If he would take responsibility for what he did, not only would he receive my forgiveness, he would find his freedom. He would be free from the secret. Its power over him would be destroyed in an instant, and he would be free to access the help he needs to overcome what caused him to molest in the first place.

What do you do if you have been hijacked by appetites you do not know how to harness and can't tell anyone about? Things might have been awakened in you that never should have been. Sexuality is meant to be a gift; but when it is awakened in the wrong environment, it destroys people. Song of Solomon 2:7 says, *"Promise me...not to awaken love until the time is right."* Perhaps someone interfered with your sexuality. He or she may have shown you images that you were never meant to see or introduced you to experiences you were never meant to know. The person may have awakened appetites at the wrong time, in the wrong place, and robbed you of your manhood or womanhood. You became a slave to your sexuality, instead of it being a gift in your life. You tried to wash yourself with water, but you never feel clean. That is the power of sin; it haunts our lives. Psalm 51:2-3 reads, *"Wash me clean from my guilt. Purify me from my sin. For I recognize my rebellion; it haunts me day and night."* The good news is that God's Word has the power to wash and cleanse you. Psalm 51 continues in verse 7, *"Purify me from my sins, and I will be clean; wash me, and I will be whiter than snow."* Daily you can allow your life to be washed by God's Word.

Once forgiven, you must determine not to feed those appetites any longer. It is foolish to set yourself up to try to resist temptation with your own human strength. Find the professional help you need. Starve yourself of everything that led you down that path or reminds you of that path. Colossians 3:5-8 tells us, *"And that means killing off everything connected with that way of death; sexual promiscuity, impurity, lust, doing whatever you feel like whenever you feel like it, and grabbing whatever attracts your fancy. That's a life shaped by things and feelings instead of by God. It's because of this kind of thing that God is about to explode in anger. It wasn't long ago that you were doing all that stuff and not knowing any better. But you know better now, so make sure it's all gone for good: bad temper, irritability, meanness, profanity, dirty talk"* (MSG). If that means there are movies, magazines, conversations, places, activities, or friends you have to give up—do it. Your life is worth more than any of those things.

"God's Spirit is on me; he's chosen me to preach the Message of good news to the poor, sent me to announce pardon to prisoners and recovery of sight to the blind, to set the burdened and battered free, to announce, "This is God's year to act!..." (Luke 4:18-19 MSG). The lie, "You can never tell," is just that—a lie. The freedom I have been talking about all along is just as much for you as for anyone. Secrets do not fall into some other class of hijacker that can never be confronted. The reign of a secret is meant to be overthrown just like the reign of all other hijackers.

Take your stand today. With the secrets out in the open, the love of God can come into your heart. And with love, the torment of the secrets ends. First John 4:18 says, *"...love turns fear out of doors and expels every trace of terror..."* (AMP).

Secrets? *I don't think so.*

Chapter 19

A NOTE TO THE HIJACKER

H is pain goes back a long time, longer than he can remember—the pain of abandonment—the pain of the person he needed the most leaving him. He has never been able to get over it. Oh, it makes sense; he can rationalize it, but deep inside it still cries out, making him wonder what was wrong with him that the person couldn't love him the way the person should have.

It left a deep wound in his soul. He fears being abandoned ever again. As a result, he feels driven to monitor the relationships in his life. He sets up house rules and keeps those closest to him under close watch. He never lets them make their own choices because if he did, he believes they might abandon him, too. He thinks that if he keeps them contained, they will never have the courage to leave. At times his fear is nearly overwhelming, and he is exhausted by the constant need to keep watch. It's not that he never lets them out of his sight. He doesn't keep them in a cell. It's more like he keeps them in a prison yard where there is an illusion of freedom, but he closely monitors the perimeter to ensure that no one crosses the invisible line of his rules. It's a wall he has built with blocks of cruel words, harsh accusations, and sometimes even physical blows. It controls his loved ones the same way an electric fence does. To someone who doesn't know it is electric, it looks harmless; but to anyone who has experienced its fury, it is something to be avoided at all costs. Even with that much control in place, he doesn't feel safe. If anyone dares ask him to stop the abuse, he believes the person is rejecting him. The words burn like salt poured into an open wound. He cannot recognize the pain and he rages back, doing everything in his power to shut the family member up. He has to maintain control at all costs.

In relationships outside his family, if he senses any distance, he withdraws. He determines to leave them before they leave him, but in his mind he blames them for rejecting him. He is terrified of being abandoned, and yet his illogical behavior continually drives people away. He makes relationships nearly impossible. The abandonment he experienced in his childhood, long since ended, has hijacked him.

Just like I did, he became a victim. What should have been restricted to a bad experience became a life sentence. He believed the lie that the abandonment was about him, and he embraced a victim mentality. The difference between him and me is that while I became a victim in my relationships, he became an abuser in his. Instead of ruling over the abandonment, he chose to rule over someone else.

I became a victim; he became an abuser. He serves abuse for the same reason I did—because of the way he thinks. We are just different sides of the same coin. Usually when people are mistreated or abused, they will make one of two choices. They will either become victims of more abuse, or they will become abusers, imitating what was done to them. *A victim assumes a role of powerlessness; an abuser assumes a role of power—but the groundwork is the same in both cases.* The deciding factor in the outcome can be as simple as whether the person's temperament is passive or aggressive. My responses to childhood events became stepping stones into abusive situations. A hijacker's responses became stepping stones to becoming an abuser. He became an abuser the same way I became a victim; *he thought so.*

If you are a hijacker, if you have taken control of the lives of others, then this chapter is for you. Perhaps somewhere, sometime, somehow you were mistreated. Maybe you were abused, violated, or raped. Were you abandoned, rejected, or blamed for something you had no control over? Perhaps you were made to be responsible for something you weren't capable of being responsible for. Maybe you had to be the parent to your own parent who functioned like a child. Perhaps something was taken from you. Your innocence? A parent? Your dreams? Your childhood? Maybe you have felt pain for as long as you can remember, and you don't even know where it came from.

We are not a lot different, you and I. We have both served the same master and both reaped the same reward—destruction. Abuse may have cost you your marriage, your children, your reputation, your job, or any number of things. And yet you continue on, month after month, year after year. Your motto seems to be, "That's my story and I'm sticking to it." Your story can change.

If you've ever watched movies with hijackings in them, you will have noticed that hijackers have some things in common. They believe they have been wronged or that someone has pushed them too far. They have determined that someone owes them, and they are going to collect. Often it doesn't matter to them from whom they collect. They decide that the way to right the wrong is to take control of the lives of others and demand what they want. Hijackers have their own terms that supersede all other laws or authority; and by using a weapon of some kind, they make their demands. Everything is all about them. They believe in their hearts they are right, and so they either fail to see the effect that they have on their hostages or they see it but are undeterred by it.

People who have chosen to abuse follow the same pattern. No matter what the incident was that took them captive, they likely experienced intense pain, fear, anger, shame, or pride. They have been pushed too far and they are pushing back. They may have determined that someone owes them; and as a result, every relationship becomes a place where they unconsciously try to collect on their debt or retaliate. They fail to realize that no one can ever make up for what they have suffered. They take whatever they want in any situation, ignoring boundaries because they believe they are entitled. It is seldom a devious, calculated way of living. More often it is just the story the family has been telling for generations. They are just taking their turn. In their hearts, they believe they are right; in other words they are deceived.

The Bible doesn't just talk about sin; the Bible also talks about iniquity. Iniquity is deception in the heart. Not only is sin involved, but people's hearts are deceived about it. They do not even know they are doing it. Iniquity is a generational influence that grows in power as it passes from generation to generation, controlling the lives of its victims. Hijackers do not necessarily know that they have hijacked someone's life. Just because someone is an abuser does not mean that they intend to abuse.

Hijackers guard their pride with control. They protect themselves from being vulnerable with control. They protect themselves from pain and fear with control. They get their needs met through control. They may control their spouse, their children, their employees, or everyone around them. As a result, they exchange relationships for hostages. When people are too afraid to stand up to them or challenge them, they mistake their silence for disinterest. If they can recognize the fear, they probably do not realize their actions are the cause of it.

Hijackers make up their own rules without regard to authority, morality, legality, or ethics. They feel entitled to demand that everyone live on their terms because it is all about them. Anyone who steps into their world has to come into line or face their wrath because they must be in control at all times. Hijackers submit to no one, and they change the rules as it suits them. They think that is what they are supposed to do. Pride tells them that when someone questions them or disagrees with them, they are being disrespected, and that provokes their wrath.

You can't carry out a hijacking without a weapon. There must be some kind of threat in order to take someone hostage and keep them that way. Abusers usually have several weapons with which they exert their control. One weapon is silence. A hijacker puts people in their places by refusing to speak to them. They withhold their love, affection, and attention as a means of manipulation and control. Rage is a common weapon that hijackers use any time they feel threatened. When someone does something that touches their point of pain, whether it is fear of abandonment or feelings of inadequacy, they rage. When someone bruises their ego, they rage. When anyone tries to address the real issues or what the hijacker is afraid of, the hijacker roars like a lion, threatening to devour until the person backs off.

Along with rage comes vengeance. Rage is mostly used to instill fear, but vengeance is used to inflict pain. Any situation where hijackers feel vulnerable gives them license to become vengeful. The pressure of the pain they feel becomes too great to bear, and they unleash it on someone else. They might use physical force, or they might use words. When they do not get what they want, they simply increase the intensity of their attack. It becomes like a drug because it relieves the hijacker's pain, but its relief is only temporary because with it comes with the side effect of guilt. Guilt creates more pain and the cycle begins again.

They hate weakness in the emotions of the people around them and when they express them, hijackers attack with vigor, mocking, accusing, and impaling them as deeply as possible to get back in control of the situation. Hijackers can't see the people bleeding from the wounds of their words; they only feel the relief of having silenced them. They may feel justified in shaking someone or hitting someone if words are not sufficient to get the person to behave the way they want. Justification is another weapon of choice. Hijackers justify and defend their behavior no matter what, shielding themselves from all responsibility.

The weapons of a hijacker are weapons of self-destruction; every time hijackers use one of them, their hearts harden a little bit more and become more deceived. Eventually they may become just like a hijacker on a television show who has no sense of or feeling for anyone around him. They lose their ability to empathize or see the pain they inflict. If they can see the pain, they don't realize they are the cause of it.

If you have hijacked the lives of your family, then you probably cannot see beyond yourself. You don't know that the people in your life walk on eggshells around you, never knowing what might set you off. Your anger does not make any sense to them, because they don't know what it is you are trying to protect. They have no idea that your behavior is driven by pride or pain or fear. Their efforts to please you are futile because your rules are always changing. When they try to confront your behavior, they may genuinely want to help, but you see it as an attack against you.

No matter how innocent a request is that they might make or no matter what question they might ask, you hear it as an attack.

Those who love you, or once loved you, can only bear so much pain before they withdraw from you. When they retreat, you feel secure once again, but you have no idea the damage you have done. You may tell yourself that if they had not behaved the way they did, then you would not have had to rage at them. Truthfully, someone else's failure is seldom the real cause of your rage.

Rage can be fear-driven. You may be afraid of looking stupid or afraid of being rejected. What is it that makes you so afraid? What is it that terrifies you? Have you ever asked yourself, or are you just so used to living in fear that it is has become part of who you are? What would happen if the thing you are afraid of really did happen? Would it be as bad as you think?

The very real fear of betrayal can lie at the root of some rage. Perhaps your marriage was the best thing that ever happened to you. But one day you came home and betrayal plunged its merciless blade into your back when you opened the door to see the love of your life with your best friend. You retaliated the only way you knew how. You labeled the opposite sex as the enemy from that point onward, believing that they could never be faithful and vowing to never allow yourself to be vulnerable again. God wants you to be free from that fear. God never intended for a man or woman to bear the pain of betrayal, and it will destroy you if you live your life refusing to trust ever again. The Bible describes the real plan for married life in Proverbs 31:11, *"The heart of her husband safely trusts her…"* (NKJV). That's the quality of marriage that people are meant to enjoy.

Pride or ego can be a cause of rage. When someone pushes you too far or crosses a boundary line in your life, rage may be your way of coping. It is what you know; a default program that gets initiated whenever your pride is challenged. It might not begin as rage; it could start with intimidation and then proceed to rage if intimidation doesn't get your desired result. Once the button gets pushed, there is no turning back; a beast has been unleashed, and you will retaliate. It happens all the time. Fights break out in bars, gang members kill each other, and husbands and wives assault each other because of pride.

You may not have any idea how to respond any differently when your pride is hurt. You may never have learned how to talk things out or express your feelings and needs without using anger. This behavior may have been learned by experience but more likely was modeled to you by your parents or other authority figures. The Bible teaches that the sins of the fathers are passed to the third and fourth generation. (See Deuteronomy 5:9.) Your father or mother may have trained you in anger and intimidation, and their parents may have trained them. Proverbs 22:6 says, *"Train up a child in the way he should go, and when he is old he will not depart from it"* (NKJV). It does not say what to train a child; it just says the child will not depart from his training. We behave the way we have been trained. It is only when we recognize that we do not have to think that way that we have the opportunity to change.

No matter how much you justify, or tell yourself you are right, your justification is not valid. You are ignoring the sin and the issues in your life. You expect your justifications to satisfy everyone around you, but they do not—because what you justify, they judge. They reel from the pain you have caused them. They are wounded and they need an apology, but it never comes because all you know to do is justify. Every time you do, you rub salt in their wounds.

Justification comes with a high price. It blocks the flow of repentance, forgiveness, and healing, insisting what was done was right. It's not that people are not willing to let you start over or forgive; it is that you are not willing to confess or apologize. You wonder why they don't just get over it, but they can't move on; they don't know how.

While being in control gives you a sense of safety, it actually makes you a victim, because it destroys your relationships. *You do not have relationships; you have taken hostages.* Relationships function on giving and receiving, so when you live outside of relationship, concerned only for yourself, you are unable to give to or receive from others. When you do give to them, you do not allow them to receive, but force it on them. Everything is under your control. The control that keeps people from hurting you also keeps you from receiving their love because control is a wall, not a filter. It shuts out everything, not just pain, and leaves you in a world of isolation.

A hijacker doesn't realize that no matter what demands are met, it won't counteract the pain. No matter how much you take, your life will feel empty because things taken never satisfy. When you live your life taking from people, you cut off what people would give you in genuine relationship with you. It is difficult for you to understand that someone would meet your needs simply because they want to.

You may be asking yourself the question, *If this is true, why didn't somebody say something?* The truth is they did. The tears running down their faces, the fear in their eyes, and the pleas they made all said the same thing, "You are hurting me. Please stop."

I'm not telling you this to make you feel badly. You feel badly enough. I am telling you because the Bible says, *"Then you will know the truth, and the truth will set you free"* (John 8:32 NIV). I'm telling you so you can be free. You have to recognize that you are a hijacker, just like I had to recognize I was a victim. The moment I did, I was forever changed. You can be changed forever, too.

Recognition is the key to freedom. When you can see what you are doing, the way of escape has just been opened to you. If you are looking for freedom, it is found in truth. The truth is that your anger or rage is not against the people you are abusing. Your anger is probably against God. In your heart, you feel that He has failed you, and you hold other people responsible for it. You need to know your heavenly Father. An experience has deceived you about who He is and what He thinks of you. You believe that He is against you rather than for you. You have been taught that He will not provide for you or protect you. It doesn't matter whether you were raised in a home where God was worshiped or a home where God was ignored. When you believe lies about who God is and what His heart is toward you, you live in deception, separated from the One who lovingly created you. Psalm 51:4-6 says, *"You're the One I've violated, and you've seen it all, seen the full extent of my evil. You have all the facts before you; whatever you decide about me is fair. I've been out of step with you for a long time, in the wrong since before I was born. What you're after is truth from the inside out. Enter me, then; conceive a new, true life"* (MSG).

It is in the heart of every man and woman to know that his or her earthly father delights in them. But maybe you feel you were a disappointment. Maybe you never got your father's attention or if you did, it seemed like he was saying that you were a failure. You took that on as a judgment against yourself. Your father may not be living anymore or part of your life, but you may have decided to continue to berate yourself in his place. No matter whether or not you had your parent's approval, you are not a disappointment to God. He would like to relate to you as His son or daughter in whom He delights. Are you willing to let Him? You do not have to live as the victim of this master of abuse any longer. Just like I did, you can choose to set yourself free. In the same way that I knelt on my living room floor and prayed, asking God to forgive me of my sins and inviting Jesus to come into my heart and be the Lord of my life, you can, too.

God wants to give you the power to have control over your actions and the Bible tells us He gives us His Spirit to help us. Turn to Him for your strength. *"God is our refuge and strength, an ever-present help in trouble"* (Psalm 46:1 NIV). Women and men equally need to know that there is power available to them to change even if abuse is the only way of life they have ever known.

When you begin to trust God, you will begin to be able to trust people. God is a Man of His Word. *"God is not a man, so he does not lie. He is not human, so he does not change his mind. Has he ever spoken and failed to act? Has he ever promised and not carried it through?"* (Numbers 23:19). God doesn't promise things and then look for an escape clause so He can say, "I didn't mean it like that." He means what He says, and He says what He means. God does not use words to seduce us, get our affections, or get our devotion and then change His mind about what He promised. When He says He wants relationship, He does. God never has any other motivation for approaching us than relationship and commitment.

Stop the hijacking. How do you do that? By letting go. Begin by putting down your weapons. Stop raging. Stop inflicting pain. Stop justifying your behavior. Just stop. You may not even know how to function without these things because you have lived with them for so long, but remember they are weapons of self-destruction. They rob you every time you use them. You might need to get some help to break this cycle, but you can begin by recognizing what sets you off. When you find yourself in that situation, walk away. When you are in control of yourself again, come back. Refuse to cooperate with the hijacking anymore.

Once the weapons have been put away, the hostages are free to go. They will find that difficult to believe. You need to tell them. Begin with an apology for the way you have treated them. Nothing can set them free quicker than hearing you say that you are sorry. They are so used to your hardened heart, that an acknowledgment of what you have done can speak volumes. Controlling them has not brought you any relief from the pain of your past, so let them go. Pull down the fence of fear around their lives and start building relationships with them.

Stop making demands. Stop taking things that don't belong to you. Start respecting boundaries and ask for things when you want them. You may need to learn to communicate again. If anger and rage are the only way you know to express your pain or your needs, you will feel like you are bound. Start listening. Start giving. In turn, people will begin to give to you the relationship you have been missing. Retract the rules that you established over the lives of your family.

Everything that was motivated by fear or anger or pride has to go. It will only be destructive. Stop changing the rules, and let your word be your word. You do not have to monitor things anymore.

The path to freedom is no different for you than it was for me. You can walk through the steps outlined in the previous chapters: "Uncovering the Lies," "Overcoming Rejection," "Face Your Enemy," and "The Power of Forgiveness." *You can turn the key of forgiveness and release yourself from the prison of the past.* Move forward into the new chapter of your life story. No more weapons. No more hostages. No more hijacking. When the desire to hijack rises up inside you, choose to respond, *"I don't think so."*

Chapter 20

BUT I KNOW JESUS

Is it possible to grow up in church and still have a victim mentality? Is it possible to have been a Christian for years and be a victim? Is it possible to be in leadership and be a victim? Absolutely. It is entirely possible to be fully engaged in church life and yet not ruling in your personal life. You might be identifying with this book, and yet be confused or discouraged, thinking to yourself, *But I know Jesus. How can I be a victim?*

The Christian life is blessed by God, meaning that He empowers us and that as a result, life is meant to work and produce for us. We are intended to be successful at what we do. Our finances should work, as should our relationships and every other area. Jesus tells us in John 10:10, *"The thief's purpose is to steal and kill and destroy. My purpose is to give them a rich and satisfying life."* That does not mean that life is problem-free, but it means we are equipped with the ability to solve or overcome problems. If there is some area of your life that never works and never gets resolved no matter how much time passes, it is quite possible that you have been hijacked in that area. You may have become a slave to something you were never intended to serve. Evaluate your life to see if any of the following descriptions apply to you:

- You never have enough money to make ends meet. You feel as though you are always broke and have no hope of getting ahead. You think you work as hard as anyone else, but no matter what you do, you don't get the same results they do. It bothers you when others succeed because you can't seem to get ahead. It may have been like this in your family for generations.

• Your marriage is mediocre at best. You are two people co-existing in the same home, but you are living in anything but wedded bliss. You disagree more often than you agree, and you don't understand how other people make it work. You have accepted the lie that marriage isn't all it is cracked up to be.

• You may have a history of broken relationships. You may have been married multiple times. You are unable to maintain relationships, and you are only friends with someone for a short time before it falls apart. You ask yourself why this always happens to you.

• Sickness of one kind or another has plagued you for years. No matter how many medicines or treatments, sickness is an ongoing way of life, and it dictates what you can and cannot do. The doctors never seem to have answers for you, and you feel like something must be wrong with you because you can't get well.

• Breakthrough is elusive. You work and work, but you never get promoted or recognized. It seems as though you are always overlooked or passed by. The opportunities are always for someone else. When opportunities or breakthroughs do come your way, they are snatched out of your hand at the last minute.

• You have some kind of addiction or disorder. You are controlled by spending, gambling, alcohol, food, drugs, or pornography. Or you may be controlled by some behavior that you cannot stop. No matter how hard you try you cannot get free.

• You are unable to put down roots or commit. You never stay in one place for very long. You are driven by a constant need to move on. If something isn't changing, you get agitated. Just when things are about to produce for you, you pull out and reposition yourself, never reaping the harvest that was about to come your way. You move from house to house, city to city, church to church, or job to job, and you really do believe the grass is greener somewhere else.

• You are one person in public and another person behind closed doors. Perhaps you have one identity in public and another identity at home. In 2005, there was a movie released, starring Brad Pitt and Angelina Jolie, called *Mr. and Mrs. Smith*. Pitt and Jolie played the role of two assassins who were married to each other. Neither of them knew that the other was an assassin. During the course of the movie, they each receive an assignment to assassinate the other one and scene after scene we see them carry out attempts on each other's lives. In public, they were the picture perfect couple. Behind closed doors, they were trying to kill each other. Maybe your life is like that. Your family arrives at church looking like the model family who everyone wants to be like. They don't know that you played Mr. and Mrs. Smith all the way to church.

How can this go on in the lives of Christians? It is a question that gets asked all the time.

Salvation is the beginning of a relationship with Jesus. As that relationship grows and we mature, our lives develop into His likeness. People receive the power to rule over their lives when they receive Christ, but that doesn't mean they automatically do. In fact, they often are not even told that they should be in charge of their lives. Since we cannot do what we have not been taught, it is entirely possible to be a Christian victim. That does not mean there is anything wrong with our relationship with Jesus; it means we have a wrong way of thinking. Once we recognize our victim mentality, we can begin to change our thinking immediately. Colossians 2:6 says, *"My counsel for you is simple and straightforward: Just go ahead with what you've been given. You received Christ Jesus, the Master; now live him..."* (MSG).

It may be difficult to reconcile this. You may think you know the Bible and live according to God's ways so how could it be possible to think wrongly? The Bible tells us that the traditions of humanity make the Word of God of no effect (see Matthew 15:6 NKJV). That means the way we think can overpower the Word of God in our lives. If you think like a victim, that can cause your marriage to fail or your finances to fail or your health to fail—even though you love Jesus. Colossians 2:8 says, *"Don't let anyone capture you with empty philosophies and high-sounding nonsense that come from human thinking and from the spiritual powers of this world, rather than from Christ."* We get robbed of life when we believe things that are not in accordance with God's Word. You might argue, "But all my friends think that way." Just because something is popular doesn't make it right. The Word of God is the only standard by which we can accurately test our thinking.

So how do you change? You overcome your victim mentality by going through the same process outlined in this book as everyone else. Begin to renew your mind by examining your life to identify the lies that you have believed. They have to be exposed in order for truth to come in. You may want to sit down with a trusted friend who knows you well and ask your friend for some honest feedback about areas of your life. Do not get offended at what he or she has to say; you need honesty to help you see things the way they really are.

Second, recognize the areas in which you have been playing the victim instead of the ruler. If you find it difficult to know, then ask yourself what it is you complain about. Your complaints will point you in the right direction. It isn't necessarily present in every area of your life, but even one is too much. Why settle for a good marriage and an addiction? Why be healthy and broke? Many people settle, focusing on what they have and ignoring where their lives don't work. It is not God's way. Dominion is God's way. Decide that you are going to rule in your life. Stand up and take your rightful place as the ruler. Decide to be in charge of your finances, your health, your marriage, your future, or any other area in which you have been victimized. Face things head-on and stand your ground against wrong thinking as you process change.

Ask yourself if you have truly overcome rejection or if it is a foundation to your behavior.

Are there people you haven't forgiven? This isn't a complicated question. Your friends know because you voice it to them. Just listen to yourself. *You can't be in charge of your life if something someone did to you is controlling you.* You might have truly been wronged, but if you have justified your unforgiveness, you have blocked off God's ability to forgive you and shut off the avenues of supply in your life. You can't embrace the new when you're holding onto the old.

> *"And whenever you stand praying, if you have anything against anyone, forgive him and let it drop (leave it, let it go), in order that your Father Who is in heaven may also forgive you your [own] failings and shortcomings and let them drop"* (Mark 11:25 AMP).

> *"For if you forgive people their trespasses [their reckless and willful sins, leaving them, letting them go, and giving up resentment], your heavenly Father will also forgive you"* (Matthew 6:14 AMP).

Do you have a secret that has you living like a puppet on a string? Are you willing to continue living like that, or are you going to confront it?

Do you believe the Bible or do you believe something else? Do you have superstitions or traditions that override the power of God's Word in your life? Are your opinions about finances, health, your family, purity, morality and ethics based on the Bible or are they a tradition that has been handed down to you? Do you do business God's way or your own? Do you live God's way or your own? Do you treat your spouse God's way or some other way? Any area you operate independently from God's instruction is an area where you can be hijacked. Pay attention to the words coming out of your mouth; they reveal what you believe. The Bible describes this in Luke 6:45: *"...For out of the abundance of the heart his mouth speaks"* (NKJV). Recognize where you have been going your own way and abandon traditions that have been robbing you of life. Luke 12:31

says, *"Steep yourself in God-reality, God-initiative, God-provisions. You'll find all your everyday human concerns will be met"* (MSG).

What is your attitude toward God's Word? Is it essential or optional? Do you read your Bible regularly? Do you have a devotional life? You can't be empowered by what you don't access. It does not matter how many electrical outlets there are in a room, if you don't plug something into them, no power is released. It is the same with God's Word. Where are you at church when the Word is being preached? Are you in the restroom, the foyer, or are you texting or talking? Or are you listening and engaged? Do you receive the Word with anticipation or are you so familiar with it that you expect nothing from it? Are you so used to it that it doesn't move you or touch you anymore? Are you just indifferent? You are creating an atmosphere devoid of power in your life when you have no respect for the Word. Begin reading the Bible regularly. Psalm 1:2-3 says, *"Instead you thrill to God's Word, you chew on Scripture day and night. You're a tree replanted in Eden, bearing fresh fruit every month, never dropping a leaf, always in blossom"* (MSG). When we don't read the Bible, we satisfy our spiritual hunger with something else. Whatever you have been consuming in its place is probably not satisfying you and could very well be producing some undesirable results.

What is your attitude toward God's house? Do you love it or is church optional for you? Psalm 84:10 says, *"Better is one day in your courts than a thousand elsewhere…"* (NIV). What is your attitude toward worship and giving? Neglecting God's Word or God's house issues an invitation to other masters to rule over you: *"But seek first the kingdom of God and His righteousness, and all these things shall be added to you"* (Matthew 6:33 NKJV). What does seek first the kingdom of God and His righteousness mean to you? You come under the influence of whatever you put first in your life; by putting God first, you come under the right influence, the One who empowers you for success.

Do you listen? Do you seek counsel? Who does the talking when you ask for help? If you are the one doing the talking, you are not seeking counsel. You must listen in order to hear what people have to say. *"Without good direction, people lose their way; the more wise counsel you follow, the better your chances"* (Proverbs 11:14 MSG).

Are you disappointed? Did life not turn out the way you expected it to at some point? You may have let some disappointment erode your faith. You quit believing for anything, telling yourself whatever will be, will be.

What kind of words do you speak? Do they line up with the Word of God or do you allow yourself to say whatever you think or feel whenever you want to? When you speak negatively, about yourself or others, you create destruction in your life, no matter how much you love Jesus. James 3:5 says, *"A word out of your mouth may seem of no account, but it can accomplish nearly anything—or destroy it!..."* (MSG). A careless or wrongly placed word out of your mouth can do that. By our speech we can ruin the world, turn harmony to chaos, throw mud on a reputation, send the whole world up in smoke and go up in smoke with it—smoke right from the pit of hell. Words kill, words give life; they're either poison or fruit—you choose (see Proverbs 18:21).

Have you made any vows? Vows are words we speak that bind our lives. It is common when people have been hurt to try to protect themselves from future hurt by making a vow. They vow never to allow anyone to humiliate them again or never to trust anyone again or to get even. They might go on and forget about their vows, but they still exist. Vows are words that bind their lives. When an opportunity comes along that they want to pursue, they try to move forward, but they can't and they don't know why. They are bound to the words that they spoke and are unknowingly fulfilling them. You can repent of any vows you have made and ask God to forgive you. Then take authority over those words, canceling their power over you.

Do you act unrighteously and expect a right result? Some people think that anything goes from Monday to Saturday as long as they act properly in God's house on Sunday. That is not true. We will reap what we sow. Galatians 6:7 says, *"Do not be deceived: God cannot be mocked. A man reaps what he sows"* (NIV). We can't cheat, steal, lie, or break our word and produce a successful life.

Do you have a good work ethic? Proverbs 12:11 and 13:4 say, *"A hard worker has plenty of food, but a person who chases fantasies has no sense,"* and *"Lazy people want much but get little, but those who work hard will prosper."* You may have never been taught how to work properly. Evaluate your standards and decide to live within your means. Proverbs 24:27 says, *"Do your planning and prepare your fields before building your house."*

Do you honor? God expects us to honor everyone. Even when people have hurt us, we still must honor. That does not mean we have to like them or what they did to us; it means we must treat them as though they have value because they do. Dishonor is one of the most destructive forces we can unleash in our lives. It doesn't matter what else we have going for us, dishonor will poison everything if we give it a place. We cannot afford to dishonor God or people no matter what their status. Ephesians 6:2-3 says, *"'Honor your father and mother.' This is the first commandment with a promise: if you honor your father and mother, 'things will go well for you, and you will have a long life on the earth.'"*

Do you contribute? Life is a result of what we contribute, because God's kingdom is one of sowing and reaping and giving and receiving. If you are focused on what you can get instead of what you can give, your life will be extremely limited. Luke 6:38 says, *"Give, and you will receive. Your gift will return to you in full—pressed down, shaken together to make room for more, running over, and poured into your lap. The amount you give will determine the amount you get back."*

Studying the book of Proverbs is a great way to examine your thinking to see if you are living by tradition or God's Word. When you read a verse about an area of life you are trying to change, pay attention. Heed what it says. As soon as you recognize tradition that contradicts the Word of God, change it! Do it God's way. Luke 6:46-48 says, *"So why do you keep calling me 'Lord, Lord!' when you don't do what I say? I will show you what it's like when someone comes to me, listens to my teaching, and then follows it. It is like a person building a house who digs deep and lays the foundation on a solid rock. When the floodwaters rise and break against that house, it stands firm because it is well built."*

Your relationship with Jesus is a rock-solid foundation on which you can build every area of your life. Romans 12:2 says, *"Don't copy the behavior and customs of this world, but let God transform you into a new person by changing the way you think. Then you will...know God's will for you, which is good and pleasing and perfect."* There is power available to you to take charge of those areas of life that once had charge of you. *"O taste and see that the Lord [our God] is good! Blessed (happy, fortunate, to be envied) is the man who trusts and takes refuge in Him"* (Psalm 34:8 AMP). Is there hope of change for your marriage? Is there hope of turning your financial situation around? Is there hope of breakthrough? Is there hope of healing? Is there hope of having the abundance of life that Jesus came to give you? (See John 10:10.) *I think so.*

Chapter 21

CHOOSE LIFE

I understand that there are two ways to live—and the choice is mine. One way produces life; and if I choose that way, the result of my decisions will be life. The other way produces death; and if I choose that way, I won't literally die, but my soul will, and the result will be pain and destruction. In Deuteronomy 30:19, God says, *"I am now giving you the choice between life and death, between God's blessing and God's curse, and I call heaven and earth to witness the choice you make. Choose life"* (GNT).

Time magnifies the effects of our daily choices. When families choose God's way, there is a flow of life that gets stronger and stronger with each generation until it becomes just about impossible for anything but life to exist in their family. In the Bible, this is called the blessing. (See Deuteronomy 28:1-14.)

When families choose death (living the opposite of God's way), generation after generation, there is a flow of destruction that gets stronger and stronger until it becomes nearly impossible to succeed in life. The Bible calls this a *curse*. (See Deuteronomy 28:15-68.) A curse is evident when there is a pattern of alcoholism, poverty, or abuse from generation to generation. The pattern gets stronger and stronger as it continues down the family line. It becomes harder and harder for anyone to make money in a family where poverty has existed for generations. It becomes harder and harder for anyone to be free from alcoholism where it has existed for generations. It becomes harder and harder to sustain a marriage where divorce has existed for generations.

When people begin to live in a way that is ungodly, there may be few visible consequences of the sin manifested in their lives. Using an analogy of a river, it is as though they have stepped into a stream that is only a few inches deep. The effect of their sin in their lives is minimal; their feet get wet, but their steps remain solid and they rule over their lives quite successfully. As the influence of their ungodly ways of living is passed onto the lives of their children, its power grows. The stream the children are born into is not ankle-deep; it is knee-deep and has developed a bit of a current. Occasionally, the force of the stream causes the children to lose their footing, but since they can quickly regain control, there is an illusion that they are standing on somewhat solid ground. If they step in the wrong place, they can stumble but they can get up again. By the time grandchildren are born, the stream has grown into a waist-deep, rapidly flowing river; and as a result, the grandchildren will live their lives faltering at every turn.

When the fourth generation is born, they find themselves swept up in a raging river carrying them into destruction, and they are powerless to do anything about it. This generational influence that grows in power is what the Bible calls iniquity. Exodus 20:5 says, *"you shall not bow down to them nor serve them. For I, the Lord your God, am a jealous God, visiting the iniquity of the fathers upon the children to the third and fourth generations of those who hate Me"* (NKJV).

For many generations my family had been living in ways that produced death. I am not saying they were bad people; I am saying that the ways they chose to live were not God's ways. Their thinking was not God's way of thinking. Their choices were not based on God's Word, and the result was that I felt like I was living in a river that flowed in a current of destruction. My feet couldn't touch the bottom, and repeatedly the current swept me under. It literally carried me with it, and I was powerless to go any other direction. I was ruled by iniquity. But the moment I invited Jesus into my heart, His power was released into my life so that I could stop being carried by that river. The river did not instantly stop flowing, but I stopped being carried by it. At times, it was difficult to keep my balance because I could still feel its force around me, but as I continued to choose to think according to God's way, the way that produces life, the flow of death around me slowly began to reverse. Eventually the river began to flow in the opposite direction and each day became less of a struggle. Instead of feeling as though I was fighting for my life, I began to feel empowered to live! And now, years later, what I set my mind to succeeds, and my life is fruitful and productive.

Life is the result of our choices. This means the ball is always in our court, not God's. He created the world to function according to certain laws, and we can live by those laws or oppose them. Either choice will have a consequence. The Bible calls this *"the law of sin and death"* (see Romans 8:2) and it is just as legal as the law of gravity. If you drop a rock from a building, it will fall to the ground. It does not matter whether the person dropping the rock is old or young, good or bad, godly or ungodly. The law of gravity works and so does the law of sin and death.

People live in pain, abuse, tragedy, divorce, and abandonment because they have chosen to live independently from God. God did not choose that kind of life for them. His choice is clearly stated in Jeremiah 29:11, *"'I know the plans I have for you,' declares the Lord, 'plans to prosper you and not to harm you, plans to give you hope and a future'"* (NIV). Those words were a lifeline to me as I fought my way out of a victim mentality and a cycle of abuse. It was not an easy journey; it took a lot of work and courage and determination. I had a small wooden plaque with that Scripture written on it hanging on my bedroom wall. Before I would leave my bedroom each morning, I would stop and read that Scripture, and it would give me enough strength and enough hope to carry on for that hour or sometimes that morning. Day by day, and step by step, with God's help, I broke free.

I encourage you to fight with everything in you for your freedom. I will not tell you it is easy, but captivity is not easy, either. God promises that what you are going through will not destroy you. Isaiah 43:2 says, *"When you go through deep waters [great trouble], I will be with you. When you go through rivers of difficulty, you will not drown. When you walk through the fire of oppression, you will not be burned up;*

the flames will not consume you." You can be an overcomer and not just a survivor. There is hope for you, and you can do it. And one day, if you do not give up, you will look back and realize you are not the same person you used to be. You will realize you are not a victim anymore and that your life has become worth living! You will realize that the hijackers are gone and you are free. The patterns of thinking will be broken and you will never be the same again. If you are approached by abuse, fear, addiction, disease or any number of hijackers, your answer will be simple: "I don't think so."

The decision to break free is not just for you; it will affect the lives of your children and your children's children and on down the family line. I could have stayed on the same path and been a bridge for every kind of sin and destruction that had worked in our family; but instead, I determined that I would start something different for the sake of my son. When I chose to change my mind, it was a generational choice. I chose a new kind of life for my family.

You, too, can break generational cycles. You can choose to stop telling the same story your family has been telling for generations. You can set a new precedent for all who will be born into your family line, setting them up for a life of blessing and freedom. After you are gone, if someone studies your family tree, they will say that you told a different story than anyone in your family had ever told. You broke the mold. You chose life.

I knew for certain I wanted to do everything in my power so that my son didn't have to tell the same story I had told. I wanted him to tell a story of freedom—of the dreams and destiny and purpose he would live out, not a story of captivity. In making that decision, I recognized that anything I chose to bring into my life would bring him, and eventually his children, under that influence. Just because I could do something without negative consequence to me did not mean that it would not have any consequence for him. With so many stories of alcoholism in our family, I contemplated what option I could give my son that would allow him not to tell that story. At that point in my life, I only drank on occasion and not to excess, so I did not feel that alcoholism was an issue for me. But what if it was for my son? None of my relatives who were hijacked by alcoholism set out to be controlled by it. None of them took their first drink thinking they would not be able to stop. None of them took their first drink thinking it would cost them their family or their life.

I concluded that it was not possible for me to teach my son that alcoholism was bad but a little bit of alcohol was okay. Where would that line be? How much was too much? I couldn't define the line. On that basis, I decided that the only message I wanted to give him was that there was a choice to not drink at all. I gave up alcohol completely because I wanted to do everything I could to help him from ever coming under the influence of alcoholism. I knew there would be a day when he recognized that I made a choice and I didn't ever want him to ask me the question, "Mom, why did you bring our family under the influence of alcohol? You were free not to. You didn't have to. Mom, why did you?" I never wanted to have him say, "Mom, now I'm under its influence and I can't stop."

I am not saying alcohol is bad. I could have a drink without it harming me or without feeling like I was doing something wrong. But the question, not only with alcohol, but with many of our choices is not about whether something is good or bad. The question is whether or not I want to bring my family under its influence. What will it look like? What will it look like as it continues into the next generations? You can choose not to bring your life under the influence of divorce, alcohol, pornography, unfaithfulness, gambling, or any of a number of things simply by deciding they are not options for you.

So often we make life choices by eating from the Tree of the Knowledge of Good and Evil, thinking we are either getting it right or getting it wrong. We ask questions like, "Is drinking right or wrong? Is gambling right or wrong?" That kind of questioning comes from the Tree of the Knowledge of Good and Evil, the one He commanded Adam and Eve to stay away from, because it is not a sound basis for decision making. We are meant to eat from the Tree of Life, meaning that we make choices based on what will be fruitful, productive, and life-giving. God's instruction does not say choose what's good. He said, "Choose life."

When my son was a teenager, I was well aware that time was slipping through my fingers in preparing him for adulthood. I didn't want life to be a list of dos and don'ts that could go out the window when he turned 18. I wanted to do my best to equip him to choose life for himself just as God instructed. In doing so, oftentimes when he would ask if he could do something, my response would be to ask him whether or not it would bring him life.

Whether or not he should go to a certain party or listen to certain music was not discussed in terms of what other parents were allowing their kids to do, or whether I thought it was good or bad. The discussion always came back to, "What will it produce in you?" I gave him the responsibility of answering that question so that he would own his choices. I did not want him to go through the consequences of doing whatever he wanted after I was not around to say no anymore. I wanted him to choose life for himself. One of the best lessons was when he went to a movie I specifically told him not to see. The content of the movie was not crude or immoral; it was extremely scary. I knew him well enough to know that it would produce fear in him afterward. In looking out for his best interest, I told him straight up he shouldn't go. But he wanted to. One night my phone rang as I was visiting at a friend's home. "Mom, where are you? When are you coming home?" he asked with urgency in his voice. He had just come from the movie I had told him not to see, and he was terrified. He couldn't deal with the fear the movie had produced in him. I laughed all the way home, not because I wanted him to be scared, but because it was a great life lesson for him.

I am not a victim anymore. I chose life. I am not the same person I used to be, and I would not go back to being that person for anything. I love my life, and I love my freedom. God took my sin and gave me His righteousness. He took my pain and gave me His comfort. He took the ashes of my life and gave me beauty. And He took the grief from my heart and gave me a song in its place. The prophet Isaiah says it this way: *"...He has sent me to bind up the brokenhearted, to proclaim freedom for the captives and release from darkness for the prisoners, to proclaim the year of the LORD's favor and the day of vengeance of our God, to comfort all who mourn...to bestow on them a crown of beauty instead of ashes, the oil of joy instead of mourning, and a garment of praise instead of a spirit of despair..."* (Isaiah 61:1-3 NIV).

Chapter 22

CREATING A MASTERPIECE

S alvation means nothing is broken, nothing is missing. As the good news of what Jesus has done for you permeates your entire life, it has the power to restore every area of brokenness in your life. Imagine your life with nothing broken and nothing missing. Regardless of where you are presently, the picture of nothing broken and nothing missing is the picture that should develop in your mind for your future. John 10:10 says, *"...I came that they may have and enjoy life, and have it in abundance (to the full, till it overflows)"* (AMP).

At my lowest points, in an attempt to find hope for a better life, I would look at the lives of people around me. Instead of finding hope, I would conclude that no one else had it any better than I did. Then I would tell myself, *Melanie, this is life. This is as good as it gets. No one has it any better than you, so get on with it. Ignore the pain, quit expecting change, and get over it.* What little hope I had faded away until there was no picture left in my mind at all of a different future. What was would continue to be. That is what happens when people lose hope; they lose their vision for the future. They can see nothing but darkness ahead. It reminds me of the Bible's description of creation. Genesis 1:1-2 says, *"In the beginning God (prepared, formed, fashioned, and) created the heavens and the earth. The earth was without form and an empty waste, and darkness was upon the face of the very great deep..."* (AMP). That was exactly how my life felt. Without form. Empty. A waste. A deep, dark waste. There was no light, no hope, no picture.

It was into that hopelessness that God came. When I realized that I could give my life to Christ, I had no understanding that He had come to give me a future; I only understood that He could save me. About three weeks after I had surrendered my life to Him, something unexpected happened. As I walked into a shopping mall, I suddenly felt life come into me as I took a deeper than normal breath. I felt as though I was seeing the world in color for the first time in a long time. Hope had sprung up. Salvation was working in me. I didn't know what I was hoping for, but I could feel hope. It was so good. Proverbs 13:12 says, *"Hope deferred makes the heart sick, but when the desire comes, it is a tree of life"* (NKJV).

Although hope had sprung up, I still couldn't see any vision for my future. Life was incredibly difficult as I fought my way through the overwhelming process of a divorce and a custody battle. A good day was one when the phone didn't ring and bring more devastating news. That was rare. The only picture I had for each day was one of trying to survive. I would sleep eleven or twelve hours a night and still wake up exhausted because I could only see darkness ahead. As I mentioned in the previous chapter, when I didn't know how I could face the day ahead, I would read Jeremiah 29:11: *"'For I know the plans I have for you,' declares the Lord, 'plans to prosper you and not to harm you, plans to give you hope and a future'"* (NIV). I had no idea what the plans might look like. I had no idea what the future might look like. I only knew there was light in my darkness and that gave me enough hope and enough strength to continue. I didn't realize it, but I had begun to frame my future with God's Word. Psalm 130:5 says, *"I wait for the LORD, my whole being waits, and in his word I put my hope"*(NIV).

In the story of creation, after the Bible describes the earth as an empty waste without form, it goes on to say, *"...The Spirit of God was moving (hovering, brooding) over the face of the waters. And God said, Let there be light; and there was light"* (Genesis 1:2-3 AMP). God was "hovering and brooding." I believe He was planning and dreaming and imagining. I think that He was forming the future. And then, God spoke. God spoke, and whatever He said came into existence.

Where was God when I was living in utter hopelessness? I believe He was hovering and brooding over me. I believe He was planning, dreaming, and imagining for my life. In the same way that His Word brought light to the earth, His Word was bringing light to me and forming my future.

Psalm 103:14 reads, *"For He knows our frame; He remembers that we are dust"* (NKJV). The word *frame* means "form, framing, purpose, framework, imagination, thing framed."[1] Genesis 2:7 says, *"The Lord God formed man of the dust of the ground, and breathed into his nostrils the breath of life; and man became a living being"* (NKJV). The word *formed* here essentially means to form, fashion, frame, predetermine, preordain or through the squeezing into shape.[2] In other words, we were framed, purposed, pressed, formed, squeezed into shape and imagined. We are God's masterpiece.

How do we receive the fullness of all God has for us? How do we frame our world to display the plans and the future God has imagined for us? How do we frame our world to reveal a masterpiece of salvation, with nothing missing and nothing broken? We frame it with His Word, the same way He did. We think it; we imagine it; we squeeze it into shape in our minds with His Word as the frame. I thought Jeremiah 29:11 was a lifeline, but really it was an outline. It was a frame of a hope and a future into which I was forming my life. Isaiah 26:3 reinforces this thought: *"You will keep in perfect peace all who trust in you, all whose thoughts are fixed on you!" Peace,* which means completeness, is the result of our mind, or our imagination being fixed on God's Word.[3] In the Message version, Isaiah 26:3 reads, *"People with their minds set on you, you keep completely whole…."* That describes the work of a Master craftsman. God's masterpiece is salvation—life with nothing missing and nothing broken.

Another lifeline that became an outline, a frame for my life, was the fact that I could never be separated from God's love. *"For I am convinced that neither death nor life, neither angels nor demons, neither the present nor the future, nor any powers, neither height nor depth, nor anything else in all creation, will be able to separate us from the love of God that is in Christ Jesus our Lord"* (Romans 8:38-39 NIV). I studied that verse over and over again, securing it in my mind. It brought me a sense of peace and confidence in the midst of my chaotic circumstances.

Reading the Bible sparked an insatiable appetite in me to know more about God, and I began to read it every day. God's words were the words I wanted to frame my life with. At first I clung to His Word to survive, but gradually I discovered that the Bible was actually changing me as I read. The Bible is not an ordinary book. It is alive. *"For the Word that God speaks is alive and full of power [making it active, operative, energizing, and effective]; it is sharper than any two-edged sword, penetrating to the dividing line of the breath of life (soul) and [the immortal] spirit, and of joints and marrow [of the deepest parts of our nature], exposing and sifting and analyzing and judging the very thoughts and purposes of the heart"* (Hebrews 4:12 AMP).

Here are more amazing things that I discovered about God's Word:

> It has creative power. *"And God said, 'Let there be light,' and there was light"* (Genesis 1:3 NIV).

> It lights our path. *"Your word is a lamp for my feet, a light on my path"* (Psalm 119:105 NIV).

> It washes us. *"...by the washing with water through the word"* (Ephesians 5:26 NIV).

> It is life. *"...And the very words I have spoken to you are spirit and life"* (John 6:63).

> It sets us free. *"...if you remain faithful to my teachings. And you will know the truth, and the truth will set you free"* (John 8:31-32).

> It is the bread of life. *"Man shall not live by bread alone, but by every word that proceeds from the mouth of God"* (Matthew 4:4 NKJV).

It is a weapon. *"And take the helmet of salvation, and the sword of the Spirit, which is the word of God"*(Ephesians 6:17 NKJV).

It creates faith. *"So then faith comes by hearing, and hearing by the word of God"*(Romans 10:17 NKJV).

It heals us. *"He sends forth His word and heals them and rescues them from the pit and destruction"* (Psalm 107:20 AMP).

The Bible is full of words to live by. Spending time reading it every day will change you as it becomes the framework for your life. It will free you from the lies that took you into captivity. You do not have to feel anything when you read the Bible; just allow it to become more familiar to you than any lies you have believed. As salvation frames your life, God's glory will be displayed. *"But you are not like that, for you are a chosen people. You are royal priests, a holy nation, God's very own possession. As a result, you can show others the goodness of God, for he called you out of the darkness into his wonderful light"* (1 Peter 2:9). Your life will fit into the framework you imagine. God's Word is the only framework fit for a masterpiece of salvation.

What we expect determines our experience. During the process of allowing God to create a masterpiece of my life, I realized there was a picture in my mind that I had to take down and replace with a new one—it was a picture of the Master. I found myself frustrated with the design of my life. I wanted to change it, but God would not respond to me the way I was expecting Him to respond. During this process, I realized that my picture of Him was wrong.

We are all created to serve God; He is our Master. Colossians 3:23-24 says, *"Work from the heart for your real Master, for God, confident that you'll get paid in full when you come into your inheritance. Keep in mind always that the ultimate Master you're serving is Christ"* (MSG). We are not designed to live independent of God. When we choose not to serve Him, we naively think that by doing so we can take charge of our own lives. The truth is that if we reject God, rather than being in control of our own lives, we will look for something else to rule over us. Instead of enjoying a relationship with the One who created us, and serving Him out of our hearts, we will serve other masters.

What is a master? A master is someone or something that rules over people's lives, making slaves out of them. God did not create master-slave relationships; they began in the Garden of Eden as the result of choices made by humankind. Adam and Eve's original relationship with God had only one rule—they were not to eat of the Tree of the Knowledge of Good and Evil. They were free to enjoy everything else in God's kingdom. Nothing else had any control or power over them. When Eve sinned by taking from the forbidden tree, God presented her with the devastating consequences of her choice. He told her that her desire and craving would be for her husband and that her husband would rule over her. This was not a punishment for her sin; it was a statement of cause and effect. God was telling her, "Eve, when you sinned, your nature changed. Instead of ruling over your world, you will now look for and crave a master to rule over you." *Sin, or separation from God, released a desire to be mastered.*

All of humanity was affected by Eve's choice to be independent and in charge of her own life. People were created to serve God; everything else was intended to serve people. Sin, or separation from God, reversed the order and created a desire within people to be mastered, causing people to become slaves to things that should serve them. They actually have an appetite for slavery and are driven to find something that will take charge of their lives. As a result, people serve masters of work, religion, pleasure, and money, as well as masters of abuse, addiction, fear, poverty, and disease. The masters are in charge and dictate what people can and cannot do. While it is more socially acceptable to be a workaholic than an alcoholic, both work and alcohol are cruel masters and both rob people of life.

There is a way for people to curb the desire for a master; it is turning their hearts to God. When people speak the word *Lord* for the first time, their whole world shifts. The One who created them and loves them becomes Master. When this original design of relationship with God is reestablished, people are freed and empowered to overcome every other master to which they have been a slave. As their relationship with Jesus grows, the power of their former masters wanes and can be overthrown.

One potential hindrance to the establishment of this relationship with God is that people tend to recreate the past through their expectations. They come into the relationship with baggage. They see God in the image of the authority figures they have had in their lives, positive or negative. If their authority figures were loving toward them, then they will expect God to be loving toward them; but if their authority figures were anything else toward them, then they will have the same expectation of God. They will expect Him to treat them the way their former masters—parents, teachers, or spouses—did. They may think they are serving Him when in reality they are serving a wrong image that they have of Him.

This was a challenge I faced in my quest for freedom and wholeness. One day, at a point of frustration with God when He would not behave the way I was expecting, I realized that I had assumed God would treat me the way my former masters had treated me, and He never would. People must understand that *God's only motive is love* or they will respond to Him like someone from their past. I recognized that when I had cried out to God at a point of desperation in my life, it was not because I thought He loved me or cared about me. It was not because I thought He was a good God. It was because I was desperate to survive. I was used to serving masters like that. I was used to serving masters I had to beg for compassion, masters that I continually had to prove myself to. Even though I had begun a new relationship with God, I was simply responding to Him as my new Master. I bowed down to Him, cowered before Him, and tried to prove myself to Him as I had done with my husband for so many years. But God would not respond like my old masters because He cannot respond in a way that goes against His nature.

This is what I wrote in my journal when I understood that I needed to get a new picture of Him: *"I am sorry that I expected You to master me too, to be one who lords over me rather than the One I love to call Lord. You are not my former husband, You are not my first grade teacher, and You are not the man who tormented my family. You are a perfect, loving Father. You connect through relationship, not tyranny and rejection. You will celebrate me, not mock me. You will cover me, not accuse me. I feel ashamed that I tried to exchange masters. I am remorseful that within me existed the need and the desire to be mastered. I am sorry that I acted like a slave instead of a daughter, and I am sorry that I saw You as a slave driver and not a Father."*

As I straightened out my thinking and began to see God for who He is, instead of the masters I had served in my past, my frustration ended, and I was able to receive His love. *"So you have not received a spirit that makes you fearful slaves. Instead, you received God's Spirit when he adopted you as his own children. Now we call him, "Abba, Father." For his Spirit joins with our spirit to affirm that we are God's children"* (Romans 8:15-16). I had to see God for who He really is in order to receive all that He had for me.

God is not like your former masters: *"Your God is present among you, a strong Warrior there to save you. Happy to have you back, he'll calm you with his love and delight you with his songs"* (Zephaniah 3:17 MSG).

Over time, as I got a true picture of God my Father and used His Word to frame my world, my life became more stable. I got a job and went back to work. I began to rebuild my life and make new friends. Broken things were being restored. Missing things were being returned. Salvation was working in me. Eventually I bought a new home that I was really happy about. I had never had a brand-new house before, and it was completely up to me to decorate and furnish it the way I wanted. I was so excited and so thankful for a new beginning. I bought a few new pieces of furniture and made the house as comfortable as I could. What I didn't notice was that there were no pictures on the walls, and the furnishings were very plain. It was a house, but it wasn't a home. Often my family would tease that I was the minimalist in the family, but really what they were verbalizing was that something was missing.

They were right. Something was missing, but it wasn't pictures on my walls. A shopping trip couldn't fix the problem. The bare walls of my home simply revealed the bare walls of my imagination. I still had no vision for my future inside me. I had framed my life with God's Word. I believed what He said about me and my future. I just couldn't see anything. It had been so long since I had a positive picture of any kind for my future that I didn't know how to begin. I had lived for so long allowing other people to make decisions for me that I didn't even know what I liked and didn't like. Although I was finding freedom because of all of the changes to my thinking, my life was not developing because I had no vision. I had to learn how to dream and imagine.

First of all I had to identify what I liked. I forced myself to make choices based on personal desire instead of function, fashion, or someone else's opinion. It took some time. I started with small things, like dinnerware. Then I tackled my wardrobe. I continued into big decisions like the kind of car I drove. These were huge steps in learning to dream again. I began to write sentences describing the life I envisioned for myself. As I practiced, the sentences expanded into paragraphs. I imagined how I would celebrate when my son came home to live with me. I knew in imagining these things that they might not develop exactly how I imagined them, but it didn't matter. The practice of imagining a future propelled me forward and allowed my life to develop. As I pictured things in my mind, the walls of my house began to fill up with beautiful pictures, and my house became a home. I was dreaming again. Not only did I have hope, not only did I have a frame, I could see the future I was hoping for—and I was watching it come to pass.

I work on the picture of my future continually, because what I see today is what will develop tomorrow. I challenge myself to always choose the best possible view. I see myself as a ruler, not a victim. My mind is no longer filled with the empty or dark canvases of a victim mentality. Today it is a gallery of bright, colorful pictures of my family, my friends, my work, my dreams, my purpose, and my future. I have lined the walls of my mind with beautiful pictures framed by God's Word, and I am His masterpiece. Ephesians 2:10 says, *"For we are God's masterpiece. He has created us anew in Christ Jesus, so we can do the good things he planned for us long ago."*

We must imagine. We must dream. The image we set inside us becomes the template for our future. It is vital to see the picture that we want in order for that future to develop. Each of us was created in

God's image. He gave us the power to plan and dream and imagine. He gave us the ability to envision what does not yet exist. Darkness? Hopelessness? Emptiness?

I don't think so!

ENDNOTES

1. See Strong's Concordance #03336.

2. See Strong's #03335.

3. See Strong's #07965.

THINK ABOUT IT

CHAPTERS 1 THROUGH 6

Did you experience traumatic events in your childhood? How did you respond to them? How did your family respond to them? How did their response affect you?

Did the events change your beliefs about yourself? Did the trauma take control of you in any way?

††††††

Do you ever respond to requests by saying, "Well, under the circumstances I…?" Do you repeatedly tell yourself, "This is just life"?

Is there anywhere in your life you feel like you have lost your freedom of choice? Have you ever considered that people can think their way into captivity? Do you have a desire for freedom?

I Think So:

Put your own name in this Scripture: Then _____ will know the truth, and the truth will set _____ free (John 8:32 NIV).

††††††

How do you see God? Do you think this is an accurate picture?

I Think So:

Put your own name in this Scripture: ...I came that _____ may have and enjoy life, and have it in abundance (to the full, till it overflows) (John 10:10 AMP).

THINK ABOUT IT

CHAPTERS 7 THROUGH 10

Have you ever noticed that other people respond to trouble differently than you do? Could it be that there is more than one way to think?

Are there any areas of pain in your life? Do you blame yourself for it? If pain is a signal, not an emotion, what could it be telling you?

⊷⊷⊷

Has trouble taken control of your life? In what way? Do you have a hijacker? What is it?

Is it true when you say that you have no choice? Make a list of choices that are available to you:

_____

_____

_____

_____

_____

Is it time for you to say, *I don't think so?*

Are you free to speak out when you think something is wrong? Do you trust your own feelings? Why or why not?

What lies have you believed as a result of things that happened to you? Who told you those lies? What is the truth?

_____

_____

_____

_____

_____

_____

How do you see yourself in relationship to God? How does God see you according to the Bible?

I Think So:

Put your own name in this Scripture: ...Nothing can ever separate _____ from God's love... (Romans 8:38).

Have you experienced disappointment? Are you willing to choose to trust God in that situation? Ask God to reveal His will to you out of His Word. Write it here.

_____

_____

_____

_____

_____

THINK ABOUT IT

CHAPTERS 11 THROUGH 13

Think about your day. Think about your week. Reflect on your conversations. The answers to the following questions will help you identify areas where you may have a victim mentality:

Your story:

Who is in charge in the story you are telling?

Is your story about what you are making happen or about what has happened to you?

Is it about what you've been doing, the choices you've been making, the direction you're going and the dreams you're dreaming or is it about what has happened to you and what people have done to you?

Do you ask yourself what you could change or do you wonder, *Why me?*

I Think So:

Put your own name in this Scripture: Now all glory to God, who is able, through his mighty power at work within _____, to accomplish infinitely more than _____ might ask or think (Ephesians 3:20).

Your feelings:

- What do you complain about? Is complaint a regular part of your conversations?

- Are you looking for ways to change whatever it is you complain about? Or is complaining a way of coping or relieving the pressure?

- Do you feel sorry for yourself? Do you like sympathy?

I Think So:

Put your own name in this Scripture: Don't be afraid, for I am with _____. Don't be discouraged, for I am _____'s God. I will strengthen _____ and help _____. I will hold _____ up with my victorious right hand (Isaiah 41:10).

Your relationships:

- Who are you talking to? Do other people question your relationships? Are you spending time with someone you shouldn't?

- Do you avoid situations, issues, and confrontations?

- How do you respond to suggestions of change? Do you embrace them? Make excuses? Blame others?

- Are you hiding anything? Your purchases? Activities? Conversations? Drinking? Spending? Pornography?

I Think So:

Put your own name in this Scripture: "Come now _____, let's settle this," says the Lord. "Though _____ sins are like scarlet, I will make them white as snow. Though they are red like crimson, I will make _____ as white as wool" (Isaiah 1:18).

Have you identified any areas where you have a victim mentality?

Once you have identified these areas, list the choices you have available to change things.

_____

_____

_____

_____

_____

_____

+>=+>=+>=

Do you see yourself as a ruler or a victim? Has the way other people have treated you caused you to have a case of mistaken identity?

+>=+>=+>=

What causes you to back down or lose confidence when facing a situation? Do you wrestle with guilt and condemnation?

I Think So:

Put your name in this Scripture: So now there is no condemnation for _____ who belongs to Christ Jesus (Romans 8:1).

When you sin, how do you deal with it? Do you justify it? Do you turn to your own strength? Do you turn to God?

What is it that makes you righteous?

I Think So:

Put your name in this Scripture: For God made Christ, who never sinned, to be the offering for _____ 's sin, so that _____ could be made right with God through Christ (2 Corinthians 5:21).

THINK ABOUT IT

CHAPTERS 14 THROUGH 17

D o you continually seek acceptance, yet expect to find rejection in the process? Do you allow people to be honest with you regarding your strengths and weaknesses? Do you believe that you have value even if you are flawed?

Can you think of any situations when you may have mistakenly thought that you were rejected?

Every time you feel rejected in the coming week, tell yourself, "It's not about me." See what happens.

⊷⊷⊷

Do you identify with the behaviors described in Chapter 15 regarding conflict?

Do you find yourself in situations that never get resolved? Are there areas of your life that you repeatedly avoid? Do you know how to face them?

What do you think would happen if you faced your enemy? Who could help you face your enemy?

When we confront things, we are able to let them go. List some things you could confront.

_____

_____

_____

_____

_____

_____

╾╂╼╾╂╼╾╂╼

Are you willing to change your thinking in order to live a life of freedom?

Do you have any boundaries on your thoughts or do your thoughts control you?

Are there things that influence your way of thinking that you could get rid of?

As you go through the week, evaluate your thinking by asking yourself, "Is this true, noble, right, pure, lovely, admirable, excellent or praiseworthy?" If it isn't, stop thinking about it! (See Philippians 4:8.)

╾╂╼╾╂╼╾╂╼

Forgiveness is the weapon God gives us to protect ourselves from offense. Who do you need to forgive? Name them. What do you need to forgive them for? Take the time right now to forgive them.

Do you need to forgive yourself? What for? Why not do it now?

I Think So:

Put your own name in this Scripture: _____ uses God's mighty weapons, not worldly weapons, to knock down the strongholds of human reasoning and to destroy false arguments (2 Corinthians 10:4).

THINK ABOUT IT

CHAPTERS 18 THROUGH 19

Are you held hostage by a secret? How does it control your life? What do you need to do to be free from it?

If you decide to confront the secret, who could give you some wise advice about how to go about it?

⊶⊷⊶

Usually when a person is mistreated or abused, they make one of two choices: to become a victim or to become an abuser. Did you make one of those choices?

Do you get your needs met through control? Do you make up your own rules?

Do you use the weapons of silence, rage, or justification in your relationships? Has your heart hardened as a result?

Do you know how to express yourself without using anger?

What provokes your anger? Fear? Pride? How can you confront the fear or pride?

Do you desire freedom? If so, are you willing to give up the rules or demands you impose on others? Are you willing to embrace truth?

I Think So:

Put your own name in this Scripture: So, _____, get rid of all evil behavior. Be done with all deceit, hypocrisy, jealousy and all unkind speech (1 Peter 2:1).

THINK ABOUT IT

CHAPTERS 20 THROUGH 22

When did you receive Christ as your Lord and Savior? Have you learned to have dominion over your life?

Is there an area of your life that doesn't work or get resolved no matter how much time passes? Can you identify a victim mentality in this area?

Do you live life God's way or your own way? Begin to read a chapter of the book of Proverbs every day and apply what you learn to your life.

◦►◦►◦►

What kinds of choices are you making? Are they based on what you think is good or bad or are they based on what they will produce?

Have you been choosing life or death? Has your family been choosing life or death?

What are you choosing to bring your family under the influence of? What do you wish your parents or grandparents had not brought your family under the influence of?

Would you like to tell a different story from the one your family has been telling for generations? What story do you want to tell?

I Think So:

Put your own name in this Scripture: Today I have given _____ the choice between life and death, between blessings and curses. Now I call on heaven and earth to witness the choice _____ makes. Oh, that _____ would choose life, so that _____ and his or her descendants might live! (Deuteronomy 30:19).

⊹⊹⊹

How do you relate to God? Do you expect that His motive toward you is always love? Do you trust Him to be good to you? Do you know that He hears you? Or do you expect Him to take from you or abuse you? Do you expect only silence when you call Him? Is He a God of love or a God dictated by your past?

Do you see God as just another master to be served? Or do you see yourself as His son or daughter?

What pictures are hanging on the walls of your mind? Would you want anyone to see them? Why not choose the best possible view? What would you like your view to look like?

I Think So:

Write your own name in this scripture: "For I know the plans I have for _____," declares the Lord, "plans to prosper _____ and not to harm _____, plans to give _____ hope and a future" (Jeremiah 29:11 NIV).

YOUR STORY

If your life has been changed by my story,
I would love to hear about it.
Please share it with me by emailing
melanie@idontthinkso.ca.

Additional copies of this book and other book titles from EVANGELISTA MEDIA™ and DESTINY IMAGE™ EUROPE are available at your local bookstore.

We are adding new titles every month!

To view our complete catalog online, visit us at:
www.evangelistamedia.com

Follow us on Facebook
(facebook.com/EvangelistaMedia)
and Twitter (twitter.com/EM_worldwide)

Send a request for a catalog to:

Via della Scafa, 29/14
65013 Città Sant'Angelo (Pe), ITALY
Tel. +39 085 4716623 • Fax +39 085 9090113
info@evangelistamedia.com

"Changing the World, One Book at a Time."

Are you an author?
Do you have a "today" God-given message?

CONTACT US

We will be happy to review your manuscript for the possibility of publication:

publisher@evangelistamedia.com
http://www.evangelistamedia.com/pages/AuthorsAppForm.htm